Great Curries

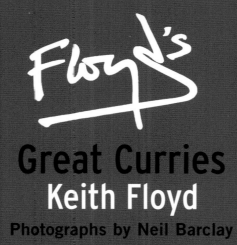

Great Curries
Keith Floyd

Photographs by Neil Barclay

CASSELL ILLUSTRATED

This book is dedicated to the memory of my mother, the best cook ever:

'Win' Phyllis Lorraine Floyd
22 November 1918–24 July 2002

With special thanks to Tess Floyd and Barbara Dixon (who has so
patiently edited so many of my books).

First published in Great Britain in 2004 by Cassell Illustrated,
a division of Octopus Publishing Group Limited,
2–4 Heron Quays, London E14 4JP

A CIP catalogue record for this book is available from the
British Library.

ISBN 1 84403 204 3

Photography: Neil Barclay
Editors: Barbara Dixon and Robin Douglas-Withers
Art direction: Jo Knowles
Design: DW Design
Stylist: Malika

Keith Floyd is represented by Stan Green Management, Dartmouth,
Devon; telephone 01803 770046; fax 01803 770075;
email sgm@clara.co.uk; visit www.keithfloyd.co.uk

Cassell Illustrated would like to thank David Mellor and Paperchase
for the loan of some of the props used in this book.

Printed in China

Contents

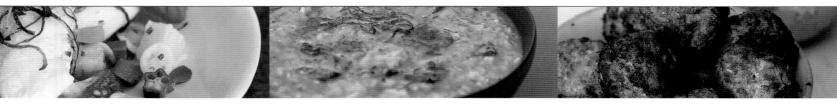

Introduction

My mother was a great gardener and a great cook. Every morning she would tend to the garden, the front with its flowers, and the back where there were neat rows of runner beans, broad beans, potatoes, cabbages, carrots, parsnips, purple sprouting broccoli and, in due season, spring onions, radishes and lettuces. Most of the vegetables she grew from seed. The little patch at the bottom contained tubs of mint and horseradish. There was sage and parsley, thyme and rosemary; there were apples and plums.

After I'd left home, whenever I visited my mother a feast would be waiting. She would say, 'I wasn't sure if you would prefer duck or roast leg of lamb with onion sauce, so I have prepared both!' My mother was not one to use gravy granules. The gravy for the duck was made from its giblets, feet, etc., and the gravy for the lamb was made from the roasting juices and vegetable water. Each had its distinctive, natural flavour.

Oh yes, God bless my dear old mum. Her passion and love for food was unrivalled and without doubt it was my mother's cooking that irrevocably influenced my life and ultimate career. We all miss her terribly – she died in 2002, aged 84.

In her larder there were no jars of shop-bought brandied jams, preserves or pickles, just a row of little muslin-topped jam jars, with stuck-on handwritten labels, for piccalilli and apple jelly, and screw-topped jars of home-pickled onions, or home-made blackberry and apple or raspberry jam, for spreading on thick slices of bread and butter at teatime. And, of course, much, much more.

But although, with a few exceptions such as cocoa and tinned salmon, there were no shop-bought items in the larder, there was one tin that contained an ochre-brown coarse powder and bore the legend 'Madras Curry Powder'.

Throughout the week, and week by week, dinner was a rotation of home-made faggots and peas, boiled ham with butter beans and parsley sauce, belly of pork with purple sprouting broccoli or curly kale and boiled breast of lamb with caper sauce; on Friday nights we always had braised pigs' trotters served with coarse salt, pepper and vinegar and thick slices of bread (no butter because the trotters were so fatty and gelatinous it was not required); sometimes on a Monday a shepherd's or a cottage pie made from the leftover Sunday joint, and then, sometimes, and particularly after Christmas, when the turkey had been served hot on Christmas Day and cold on Boxing Day, the ubiquitous Madras curry powder would come out and pieces of cooked turkey, lamb or beef were stirred into this gritty, ochre-coloured sauce. Curry, it was called! Served with boiled rice with side dishes of desiccated coconut, banana slices, sultanas and apple chunks. It was truly revolting. This awful meal would occur at least once a month, but it intrigued me. What was a curry? And then after I started working and joined a local rugby club, I soon discovered the world of Indian restaurants and the Saturday night culture of pints of lager with a Vindaloo. Nowadays, of course, the curry is a thousand times removed from what pleased us all those years ago.

The good thing about curries is that they are really simple and quick to prepare and fun to eat. For the most part they can be

prepared and frozen for future use and they make great party food – a table groaning with seven or eight different dishes, a range of pickles and chutneys, yoghurts and fresh herbs, wonderful breads, lashings of cold lager or ginger beer or fresh lime juice with sparkling water, jugs of salted or sweetened lassi or maybe just cups of green tea. What a party!

And you don't have to be fussy about measuring or weighing ingredients. Cook with your eyes, taste as you cook, dip your finger in. More chillies to make it hotter? Add more chillies. Too hot? Stir in more cream or yoghurt. The hottest chillies, used in many of the recipes in this book, are known as bird's eye chillies – they are very small and very, very hot. The bigger the chilli, the milder it is. If you leave the seeds and pith in the chilli, it is hotter; with these removed, the dish will be milder. If in this book the recipe calls for chicken, you don't have to follow that slavishly – you can use lamb, or pork, or beef, or quail! Curries are a moveable feast.

So, here you will find contained over 30 years' worth of hurtling round the globe, learning and enjoying these, some of my favourite curry recipes.

Happy cooking, and may all the wonderful aromas, spices and flavours of the Orient be with you.

Keith Floyd
Isle sur la Sorgue, France

Curry Culture

At 16 I left school, managed to get a job and joined a local rugby club. On Saturdays we would play our game in some lowly division and immediately after the match rush down to the memorial ground in Bristol to watch Bristol Rugby Club thrash any of the top teams in the country. There was always someone who would get us into the clubhouse bar after the game where we could be close to our heroes.

We drank pints and pints of cheap lager until someone said, 'It's time for a curry.' Up until then I had never been to an Indian restaurant and I was possibly the youngest member of our side, so ten or twelve of us would invade the Taj Mahal or the Koh-I-Noor – plain, simple places with stained flock wallpaper, Formica tables covered with an invariably equally stained white tablecloth, with cheap glass salt and pepper shakers and a chrome bowl filled with white sugar lumps. This was in the late 1950s to the early 1960s.

The owner wore a rusty dinner jacket, the shy waiters wore white jackets. There was Chicken or Beef Madras, Vindaloo and not much else – a few European dishes such as T-bone steaks and omelettes; there was mango chutney and poppadoms – oh, and Bombay Duck, deep-fried smelly dried fish. We would order the hottest dish – in those days there was no raita, no buttered Indian breads, certainly Chicken Tikka Masala had not been invented, which, by the way, to this day does not exist in India. There were none of the subtle dishes that we know today. Certainly there was no such thing as a Thai or Malaysian restaurant. The only other curry you might get would be in a Chinese restaurant: a piece of chicken with a hot sauce, not dissimilar to the one my mother made, and often served with chips.

I suppose it was fun and I suppose we enjoyed it, but it wasn't real. Time has moved on. The tandoor oven came to Britain and subtler flavours and tastes emerged. The derogative term 'curry house' slipped into obscurity and fine designer Asian restaurants began to appear. Supermarkets introduced ranges of Asian food to cook or reheat at home and curry became big business.

You will find curries, as far as I know, a British-invented term for spicy dishes; certainly there are no 'curries' in India, but there are curries in Malaysia, Thailand, Burma, Africa – in fact all over the world, all created through interpretation, taste, geographical location and the availability of spices and produce.

The spicy dishes in this book come from my travels in those countries, and in India, Vietnam, Kashmir, Egypt (yes, they have curries) and many other places. Some are wet, some are dry; 'curry' is sometimes loosely defined – as in Vietnamese Meat Loaf, a highly spiced meat mixture with fish sauce and chillies – and sometimes immediately recognisable, as in Thai Green Chicken Curry or Lamb Rogan Josh.

The curry has certainly moved on from the lager and Vindaloo days, and we are now able to enjoy many styles of these spicy dishes, as will be seen from the variety and diversity of the recipes in this book.

Spices and Equipment

Essential ingredients of curries, like ginger or galangal, garlic, onions and chillies, are really good for you – good for the blood, good for your digestive system. And it's brilliant that so many of the ingredients that were once so hard to find – like curry and lime leaves, lemon grass and shrimp paste – are now available in most supermarkets.

If you are buying powdered spices, don't keep them in the storecupboard for months as they'll become stale and tasteless.

Better to go to an Asian shop and buy them loose and fresh, just what you need for any particular meal or, if you are going to be purist, and I hope sometimes you will have the time to be so, buy your peppercorns, coriander, cloves, star anise and cardamoms whole, crush them and toast them very lightly in a dry frying pan before you mix up your curry paste or masala, as the Indians call it.

Buy your ginger and lemon grass in small amounts, grow some fresh herbs to pick when you need them, and make your own ghee or clarified butter as and when you need it. Freshness is everything for a good curry.

And a word about chillies – the smaller the chilli, the hotter it is. It's up to you if you want to use them with the seeds and pith intact, but removing these will tone down the fire a little.

You don't need specialist equipment to cook curries. They're not cooked in heavy casseroles in the oven for hours; in the main they are cooked in heavy-bottomed sauté or frying pans, or heavy woks.

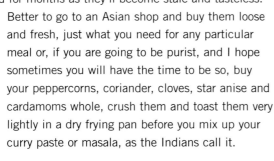

Stir-frying implements and slotted spoons are handy, as are blenders or food processors.

Before you start cooking your curry, equip yourself with a load of rectangular, plastic boxes or small, glass bowls. Read your recipe carefully. Chop and prepare all your ingredients and place them individually in your bowls in the order in which you add them to the dish. Don't start frying the chicken and then begin to peel the onions. Careful preparation, which can be done hours ahead of cooking time, will ensure that you, as well as your guests, have a good, stress-free time.

The observant among you will notice that I have always put the main ingredient of the recipe first in the ingredients list, and not necessarily in the order in which it is used – this is to remind you when you make your shopping list! A chicken curry isn't much good without the chicken.

A final word of advice. Except when I make my mother's Christmas cake and her Christmas puddings, I never use scales. All the measurements, weights and cooking times in this book are approximate. Don't follow them slavishly, use common sense, and if you are not already an experienced cook, just rely on a bit of trial and error.

The recipes will generally serve 4–6 people, depending on how hungry you are.

Chicken Curries

This makes a change from good old plain roast chicken.

14 | Vietnamese Roast Chicken with Lemon Grass and Tangy Sauce

1 roasting chicken about 1.5–1.75 kg/ 3 lb 5 oz–4 lb

3 stalks of lemon grass

6 garlic cloves, peeled

4 shallots, peeled

2 fresh red chillies, deseeded

1 tablespoon sugar

1 tablespoon fish sauce

½ teaspoon salt

a good handful of fresh coriander leaves, chopped, to garnish

For the tangy sauce

2 garlic cloves, peeled

1 fresh red chilli, deseeded

2 tablespoons sugar

2 tablespoons fresh lime juice

2 tablespoons red wine vinegar

2 tablespoons fish sauce

Serves 4–6

First make the tangy sauce by whizzing all the ingredients together in a food processor, then set aside.

Preheat the oven to 220°C/425°F/mark 7. Put the lemon grass, garlic, shallots, chillies, sugar, fish sauce and salt into a food processor and whiz until you have a paste.

Using your hands, loosen the chicken skin on the breast and legs and rub half of the lemon grass paste onto the chicken, under the skin. Rub the remaining paste over the chicken skin and into the chicken cavity.

Put the chicken on a roasting rack and roast in the oven for 15 minutes, then reduce the heat to 190°C/375°F/mark 5 and continue to roast for about 1¼ hours, basting the bird regularly with the cooking juices from the bottom of the pan.

Before serving, rest the chicken for 10 minutes.

Carve the chicken into portions, garnish with the coriander leaves and serve with the sauce.

In Asia coconut is used extensively in cooking. It adds a wonderful flavour and texture to so many dishes. Coconut milk is now, luckily, widely available.

Dry Chicken and Coconut Curry

500 g/1 lb 2 oz bite-sized chicken pieces on the bone (or, if you don't like bone, diced chicken breasts)

a 400 ml/14 fl oz tin of coconut milk

For the curry paste (or masala, as the Indians call it)

2.5 cm/1 inch piece of fresh ginger, peeled and chopped

grated zest of 1 lime

½ teaspoon shrimp paste

6 garlic cloves, peeled and chopped

1 bunch of fresh coriander leaves (use the stalks for this paste and save the leaves for the garnish)

3 shallots, peeled and chopped

1 stalk of lemon grass, chopped

2 fresh green chillies, chopped

1 heaped teaspoon mixed caraway and coriander seeds, coarsely crushed in a pestle and mortar

Serves 4–6

Put all the ingredients for the curry paste into a food processor and whiz to a purée.

Heat the coconut milk, add the chicken pieces and simmer gently until the chicken is tender. If during this process the coconut milk is getting too thick, add a little water.

When the chicken is nearly cooked, stir in the curry paste and continue cooking gently until the chicken is richly coated with the sauce and is really quite dry.

Garnish with the coriander leaves and serve with any rice and chutneys of your choice (see pages 128–141).

A creamy, rich chicken dish thickened with a walnut paste. Plain rice would be a good accompaniment.

Red Chicken with Walnuts

1 kg/2¼ lb skinned chicken breasts, on the bone

450 ml/¾ pint chicken stock

2 tablespoons ghee or clarified butter

1 red onion, peeled and finely chopped

2 garlic cloves, peeled and very finely chopped

1½ tablespoons paprika

1 teaspoon chilli powder

100 g/3½ oz walnuts, finely ground in a food processor

300 ml/½ pint single cream

2 tablespoons walnut oil

salt

a handful of finely shredded flat-leafed parsley, to garnish

Serves 4–6

Put the chicken breasts in a pan with the chicken stock, bring to the boil and simmer for about 15 minutes or until the chicken is cooked.

Using a slotted spoon, remove the chicken breasts, reserve the stock and set both aside in a warm place.

Heat the ghee or clarified butter in a pan and fry the onion for a couple of minutes until soft but not brown. Add the garlic, 1 tablespoon of the paprika and the chilli powder. Cook for a further minute.

Add to this 225 ml/8 fl oz of the reserved chicken stock, the walnuts, cream and salt to taste and heat through, stirring well. If the mixture is a little thick, add a little more of the chicken stock.

Shred the cooked chicken and add to the sauce, stirring it well together, then place on a serving dish.

Gently warm the walnut oil in a small saucepan, add the remaining paprika and drizzle over the chicken. Serve garnished with parsley.

The addition of nutmeg to this dish gives it a uniquely savoury lift.

Chicken Breasts in a Spicy Yoghurt Sauce

4 skinned, boneless
chicken breasts

ghee or
clarified butter

2 garlic cloves, peeled
and finely chopped

2 fresh green
chillies, chopped

2.5 cm/1 inch piece
of fresh ginger, peeled
and finely chopped

1 clove, crushed

300 ml/½ pint tub of
natural yoghurt

*For the masala
(curry paste)*

ghee or
clarified butter

50 g/2 oz blanched
large almonds,
chopped

50 g/2 oz cashew
nuts, skinned
and chopped

2 red onions, peeled
and finely chopped

3–4 fresh green
chillies, chopped

1 teaspoon crushed
poppy seeds

2 bay or
cinnamon leaves

1 teaspoon
nutmeg powder

salt

Serves 4–6

To make the paste, heat some ghee or clarified butter in a frying pan and gently fry all the paste ingredients until they are lightly cooked. Add a cup of water and simmer for about 10 minutes.

Remove the bay or cinnamon leaves, put the mixture into a food processor and blend to a smooth paste.

In another pan, heat some ghee or clarified butter, then add the garlic, chillies, ginger and clove and stir-fry for a minute or so, then add the chicken breasts and fry gently on both sides until they are almost cooked.

Lower the heat and stir in the masala until the chicken pieces are well coated. Add a little water and make sure the mixture is nice and smooth. Gently stir in the yoghurt and cook slowly, so as not to curdle the sauce, until the chicken is cooked through.

x) very rich because of nuts

x) chicken breasts were whole, perhaps chop them up

x) if made again don't crush nuts too finely so that they take on some colour

Although it seems fiddly to eat, chicken left on the bone is the most tasty. Ginger complements chicken (and duck) very well and, despite its simplicity, this is a warming dish, the heat coming from the raw spring onion instead of chilli.

Ginger Chicken

1 whole free-range chicken, chopped into bite-sized pieces on the bone (or, if you are a gastronomic wimp, 4 boneless chicken breasts, cut into bite-sized pieces)

vegetable oil, for frying

3 or 4 garlic cloves, peeled and very finely chopped

5 cm/2 inch piece of fresh ginger, peeled and grated

1 teaspoon cumin powder

2 teaspoons garam masala powder

juice of 2 lemons or limes

225 ml/8 fl oz or so of chicken stock

1 bunch of fiery spring onions, finely chopped

salt and freshly ground black pepper

chopped fresh coriander leaves, to garnish

lemon wedges, to serve

Serves 4–6

Heat some vegetable oil in a frying pan and stir-fry the chicken pieces until they are golden, then season with salt and pepper.

Stir in the garlic, ginger, cumin and garam masala and stir-fry until the pieces are well coated.

Add the lemon or lime juice and chicken stock and simmer gently until the chicken is tender.

At the last minute, add the chopped spring onions – they are raw rather than cooked.

Garnish with the coriander leaves and serve with lemon wedges and saffron rice with cumin (see page 131).

To make this even richer, stir in a little double cream just before serving.

These chicken cakes are as good served cold as they are served hot.

Chicken Korma

1.4 kg/3 lb chicken, jointed

150 g/5 oz ghee or clarified butter

2 large onions, peeled and sliced

1 teaspoon chilli powder

4 teaspoons onion powder

1 teaspoon coriander seeds

2 tablespoons cinnamon powder

½ teaspoon ground ginger

10 black peppercorns

5 cloves

6 cardamom pods, ground

2 garlic cloves, peeled and crushed

1 teaspoon salt

300 ml/½ pint tub of natural yoghurt

3 bay leaves

300 ml/½ pint chicken stock or water

juice of 1 lemon

Melt the ghee or clarified butter in a large pan and fry the onions until golden brown. Remove from the pan with a slotted spoon and put to one side.

Add all the spices and the garlic to the pan and fry until brown, then throw in the chicken and salt and cook until browned.

Add the yoghurt, bay leaves and stock or water and return the fried onions to the pan. Bring to the boil, reduce the heat, cover with a tight-fitting lid and simmer for 1½–2 hours, until the chicken is tender.

Remove the pan from the heat, pour in the lemon juice and mix well. Remove the bay leaves and serve with plain boiled rice.

Serves 4–6

Spicy Chicken Cakes

approx. 500 g/ 1 lb 2 oz minced raw chicken

100 g/3½ oz breadcrumbs

2 fresh green chillies, very finely chopped

3 or 4 tomatoes, skinned, deseeded and very finely chopped

3 or 4 spring onions, very finely chopped

1 large garlic clove, peeled and crushed

2.5 cm/1 inch piece of fresh ginger, peeled and finely grated

1 small bunch of fresh coriander leaves, very finely chopped

a large pinch of cumin powder

1 teaspoon garam masala powder

1 or 2 eggs, beaten

salt and freshly ground black pepper

vegetable oil, for frying

Combine half the breadcrumbs with all the other ingredients except the oil, then roll into small balls and flatten to make little cakes.

Press the cakes into the remaining breadcrumbs on both sides and shallow-fry in the vegetable oil on both sides until golden.

Serve with any of the salads or chutneys on pages 124–125 and 136–141.

Serves 4–6

Although it may seem strange to cook a savoury dish with caramel, it is a popular combination in many parts of Asia. The sweet-savoury mixture of the sauce is very delicious.

Spicy Caramelised Chicken Pieces

1 small, free-range chicken, chopped into bite-sized pieces on the bone (use the whole chicken)

2.5 cm/1 inch fresh ginger, peeled and grated

2 fresh green chillies, finely chopped

salt and freshly ground black pepper

chopped fresh mint, basil and coriander leaves, to garnish

For the caramel sauce

110 g/4 oz caster sugar

1 small wine glass of fish sauce

4 or 5 shallots, peeled and very finely diced

Serves 4–6

To make the caramel sauce, melt the sugar gently in a heavy-bottomed pan, stirring all the time until it turns brown. Remove from the heat and stir in the fish sauce. Add the shallots, return to the heat and simmer gently until the sugar has dissolved and you have a smooth, golden sauce. Leave to cool.

Once the sauce has cooled, add the chicken pieces, ginger and chillies and simmer gently until the chicken is tender. Season to taste.

Garnish with the fresh herbs and serve with plain boiled rice.

Lemon and chicken are a wonderful combination in this lovely, fresh-tasting curry. It is not a hot dish, but is full of flavour.

Chicken with Lemon and Turmeric

1 chicken, jointed

vegetable oil, for frying

2 onions, peeled and finely chopped

4 garlic cloves, peeled and finely chopped

3 tablespoons turmeric powder

1½ teaspoons cumin powder

1½ teaspoons coriander powder

600 ml/1 pint fresh lemon juice

6 tomatoes, skinned, deseeded and finely chopped

2 cups cooked chickpeas

a good handful of fresh coriander leaves, chopped

salt and freshly ground black pepper

Serves 4–6

Heat some vegetable oil in a pan and fry the chicken pieces until they are crisp and golden.

Stir in the onions and garlic and cook until they begin to colour, then season and stir in the turmeric, cumin and coriander powders. Mix well to coat the chicken entirely, adding a little more oil if the mixture is too dry.

Cook the spices gently through for about 5 minutes, stirring so they do not burn, then add the lemon juice and stir, adding a little water if the mixture is dry.

Stir in the chopped tomatoes, season with salt and pepper and simmer gently for about 1 hour, when you should have a rich sauce.

Add the chickpeas and coriander leaves and warm through.

Serve with natural yoghurt with mint chopped into it.

Pilaf dishes are very popular in Asia. They make meat or poultry go a long way while providing a colourful, spicy, crunchy dish. The addition of saffron really boosts this already delicious recipe.

Chicken Pilaf with Pistachios and Almonds

450 g/1 lb skinned, boneless chicken meat, cut into 1 cm/½ inch cubes

200 g/7 oz unsalted butter

100 g/3½ oz blanched almonds, chopped

100 g/3½ oz blanched pistachios, skinned and chopped

2 or 3 fresh red chillies, chopped

510 ml/17 fl oz chicken stock

200–300 g/7–11 oz long-grain rice, washed and strained

a big pinch of saffron threads, soaked in a little hot water

salt and freshly ground black pepper

Serves 4–6

Heat some of the butter in a large frying pan and fry the diced chicken until golden.

Add the nuts and chillies and stir-fry for a couple of minutes, then cover with a little of the chicken stock and cook until the chicken is cooked and practically dry. Put to one side.

Melt some more of the butter in another pan and stir-fry the rice until it is well coated with the butter. Add the saffron and its water and the rest of the chicken stock and season with salt and pepper. Bring to the boil, then reduce the heat, cover the pan and simmer gently for 10–12 minutes.

Add the chicken and nuts and cook gently until the rice has absorbed all the liquid.

Remove the pan from the heat, melt in a few more knobs of unsalted butter, stir with a fork and let it stand for 4–5 minutes before serving.

This creamy, nutty dish is subtle and mild. Do splash out on a little saffron as it makes all the difference to the flavour. You should serve the chicken as soon as it is cooked or the sauce may separate.

Creamy Saffron Chicken

1 kg/2¼ lb chicken breasts, on or off the bone

juice of 1 lemon

100 g/3½ oz cashew nuts

a little milk

225 g/8 oz red onions, peeled and finely sliced

ghee or vegetable oil, for frying

4 garlic cloves, peeled and puréed

2.5 cm/1 inch piece of fresh ginger, peeled and puréed

7.5 cm/3 inch cinnamon stick, crushed

5 green cardamom pods, crushed

4 cloves

300 ml/½ pint tub of natural yoghurt

a pinch of saffron threads

150 ml/¼ pint double cream

a handful of fresh coriander leaves

salt

Serves 4–6

Put the chicken breasts into a bowl, sprinkle with salt and the lemon juice and leave in the fridge for about 1 hour.

Soak the cashew nuts in the milk for about 1 hour, then purée with the milk in a food processor and put to one side.

Fry the onions in the ghee or vegetable oil until completely soft, then add the garlic and ginger purées and stir-fry until the mixture is slightly browned.

In another pan, heat some ghee or oil and fry the cinnamon stick, cardamom pods and cloves for a couple of minutes, then add the onion paste.

Reduce the heat and stir in the yoghurt and saffron, then add the chicken pieces and simmer for 10–15 minutes until the chicken is cooked.

Stir in the nut purée and cook for a further 5 minutes.

At the last minute, stir in the double cream and coriander leaves, heat through and serve.

There are a lot of chillies in this recipe, but with the addition of the cream, yoghurt and nuts it will not be too hot.

Pistachio Chicken Curry

1 kg/2¼ lb boneless chicken (breasts or thighs), cut into bite-sized pieces

100 g/3½ oz shelled pistachio nuts

8 fresh green chillies

5 tablespoons single cream

vegetable oil, for frying

2 onions, peeled and finely chopped

2.5 cm/1 inch piece of fresh ginger, peeled and grated

6 garlic cloves, peeled and finely chopped

¾ teaspoon garam masala powder

½ teaspoon turmeric powder

1 cinnamon stick

¾ teaspoon ground white pepper

1½ teaspoons fennel seeds

1 green tomato, finely chopped

3 tablespoons natural yoghurt

750 ml/1¼ pints chicken stock

salt

For the garnish

1 teaspoon green cardamom powder

a good handful of chopped fresh coriander leaves

Serves 4–6

Boil the pistachio nuts in a small amount of water for 10 minutes, then drain and cool. When cool, rub off any skin.

Put the pistachios with 4 of the chillies and the single cream into a food processor and whiz to form a paste.

Heat some vegetable oil in a frying pan, add the onions and cook until they are slightly brown. Add the ginger, garlic, garam masala, turmeric, cinnamon, white pepper and fennel seeds and cook for a couple of minutes.

Add the pistachio mixture and fry for a couple of minutes, then add the chicken and sauté for 5 minutes.

Add the tomato, yoghurt, the remaining chillies and the chicken stock. Add salt to taste and cook for 15–20 minutes or until the chicken is cooked through.

Just before serving, sprinkle with the cardamom powder and the coriander leaves.

This is a very simple dish to make, but the use of good, fresh tomatoes and limes, coriander and chillies makes it a definite favourite.

Chilli and Tomato Chicken

8 chicken thighs, skinned

vegetable oil, for frying

2 shallots, peeled and finely chopped

2 garlic cloves, peeled and chopped

500 g/1 lb 2 oz tomatoes, skinned, deseeded and finely chopped

1 tablespoon tomato purée

3 fresh red chillies, very finely chopped

2 teaspoons sugar

4 cm/1½ inch piece of fresh ginger, peeled and grated

3 teaspoons garam masala powder

1 dessertspoon soy sauce

juice of 2 limes

salt

a handful of fresh coriander leaves, to garnish

Serves 4–6

Make several cuts in each chicken thigh and put the thighs into an ovenproof dish.

Heat some vegetable oil in a pan and fry the shallots until softened, then add the garlic and fry for about 30 seconds. Add the tomatoes and simmer until you have a rich tomato sauce.

Transfer the tomato sauce to a food processor, and add all the remaining ingredients, except the chicken. Whiz until you have a smooth sauce, then pour the sauce over the chicken and refrigerate for 3 hours to allow the chicken to absorb the flavours.

Preheat the oven to 190°C/375°F/mark 5. Put the chicken in the oven and cook, uncovered, for about 1 hour.

Serve hot, garnished with the coriander leaves, and with a rice dish of your choice (see pages 128–132).

The sharp flavour of lemon grass infuses the chicken, while the slightly caramelised finish gives it an almost sweet and sour flavour. The chilli adds zing!

Chicken with Lemon Grass

900 g/2 lb skinned, boneless chicken breast, cut into bite-sized pieces

2 garlic cloves, peeled and very finely chopped

1 stalk of lemon grass, very finely chopped

2 tablespoons fish sauce

3 tablespoons white sugar

freshly ground black pepper, to taste

vegetable oil, for frying

1 fresh red chilli, deseeded and sliced into fine strips

Serves 4–6

Mix together the garlic, lemon grass, fish sauce, 1 tablespoon of the sugar and some pepper to make a marinade and mix in the chicken pieces. Leave in the fridge for about 1 hour to infuse the flavours.

When the chicken has marinated, heat some vegetable oil in a large pan and sauté the chicken until it is browned on all sides. Cover the pan and simmer over a low heat until the chicken is cooked – 15–20 minutes.

Heat the remaining sugar in a small pan until it melts and turns a caramel colour, but do not let it burn.

Drop in the slivers of chilli, then pour onto the chicken and stir to mix.

Serve with plain boiled rice.

In this dish, chicken is cooked in a rich tomato gravy scented with fenugreek leaves and then further enriched with cream and honey.

Chicken livers are often overlooked except for use in terrines. In fact, they have a wonderfully rich flavour and need very little cooking. However, beware: if they are overcooked, they can become bitter. Complemented by the other ingredients, they make this rich, unusual dish.

Spicy Chicken with Tomatoes and Fenugreek

800 g/1¾ lb boneless chicken, chopped into small pieces

1 kg/2¼ lb ripe tomatoes

4 small red onions, peeled

10 garlic cloves, peeled and 5 finely chopped

4 cm/1½ inch piece of fresh ginger, peeled and grated

5 fresh green chillies

5 green cardamom pods

1 teaspoon coriander powder

1 teaspoon cinnamon powder

½ teaspoon mace powder

3 cloves

vegetable oil, for frying

3 tablespoons fenugreek leaves

2 tablespoons ghee or clarified butter

150 ml/¼ pint double cream

3 tablespoons runny honey

salt and freshly ground black pepper

Put the tomatoes, onions, the whole garlic cloves, the ginger, chillies, cardamoms, coriander, cinnamon, mace and cloves in a large pan with a little water and cook on a high heat for about 5 minutes. Cool, then put the lot into a food processor and whiz until you have a smooth, red sauce.

Heat a little vegetable oil in a frying pan and fry the chopped garlic until it is just browning, then add the chicken pieces and stir-fry until they are golden.

Pour the tomato sauce in with the chicken and simmer until the chicken is cooked.

Stir in the fenugreek leaves and season.

Just before you serve the dish, stir in the ghee or clarified butter, cream and honey and heat to warm through.

Serves 4–6

Chillied Chicken Livers with Pepper, Onion and Tomato

450 g/1 lb chicken livers, cleaned and trimmed

ghee or clarified butter

2 red onions, peeled and very finely sliced

2 garlic cloves, peeled and crushed

1 red pepper, deseeded and finely chopped

1 green pepper, deseeded and finely chopped

1 fresh green chilli, very finely chopped

½ teaspoon chilli powder

3 tomatoes, skinned, deseeded and finely chopped

salt and freshly ground black pepper

Heat some ghee or clarified butter in a large frying pan and sauté the onions, garlic, peppers, green chilli and chilli powder until the vegetables are soft and the chilli has released its flavour.

Add the chicken livers and sauté for 5–6 minutes, stirring all the time.

Add the tomatoes and season with salt and pepper. Continue cooking for a further 2–3 minutes, then serve hot with a bread of your choice (see pages 133–135).

Serves 4–6

This is a stir-fry dish, as are indeed many curries, which makes it a great quick lunchtime meal. Supermarkets today sell very good curry pastes, and although purists may wish to make their own, bought ones work just as well!

Green Chicken Curry

450 g/1 lb skinned, boneless chicken breasts, cut into pieces

vegetable oil, for frying

3 tablespoons Thai green curry paste

a 400 ml/14 fl oz tin of coconut milk

3 tablespoons fish sauce

1 fresh red chilli, deseeded and finely chopped

1 fresh green chilli, deseeded and finely chopped

3 tablespoons brown sugar

a handful of fine green beans

a good handful of fresh basil leaves

4 tablespoons coconut cream, to serve

Serves 4–6

Heat some vegetable oil in a large pan or wok and stir in the green curry paste. Cook for about 30 seconds, then throw in the chicken and quickly stir-fry with the paste for a couple of minutes.

Add the coconut milk, fish sauce, chillies, sugar and beans, stir well and cook for 5–7 minutes, then toss in the basil leaves.

Serve hot, topped with a dollop of coconut cream.

You could substitute asparagus for the baby leeks if you wish: just prepare them in the same way as the leeks.

This is another typical Thai dish – very light and spicy and very simple. Bird's eye chillies are the very small, very hot chillies. If you prefer you could substitute larger chillies, cut into very fine strips.

Garlic and Coriander Chicken

Hot Chicken Salad, Thai Style

4 skinned, boneless chicken breasts

10 baby leeks

vegetable oil

fresh coriander leaves, to garnish

For the marinade

4 teaspoons coriander seeds

4 teaspoons cumin seeds

5 garlic cloves, peeled and very finely chopped

4 teaspoons paprika

2 teaspoons chilli powder

a good grind of black pepper

1 teaspoon salt

2 tablespoons vegetable oil

Serves 4–6

To make the marinade, toast the coriander and cumin seeds in a dry frying pan for a few seconds, then grind them in a pestle and mortar. Mix with the rest of the marinade ingredients and stir until well amalgamated.

Cover the chicken breasts with the marinade and put in the fridge for 30 minutes.

Brush the leeks with vegetable oil and grill or griddle until they are tender.

Grill the chicken on both sides, until golden and cooked through.

Serve the chicken on the baby leeks and garnish with coriander leaves.

225 g/8 oz skinned, cooked chicken

2 tablespoons fish sauce

juice of 1 lime

1 shallot, peeled and finely chopped

2 spring onions, finely chopped

a good handful of fresh coriander leaves, chopped

3 dried bird's eye chillies, finely ground

fresh mint leaves, to garnish

Serves 4–6

Mix together the chicken, fish sauce and lime juice.

Add the shallot, spring onions, coriander and chillies and mix well.

Serve garnished with the mint leaves.

These are great for eating with your fingers. The skin of the poussins should be nicely crisp and the meat tender and succulent. This is Indian chicken and chips!

Fried Green Poussins

2 poussins, skin on, cut in half along the breastbone and backbone to create halves

juice of 1 lime

vegetable oil

2 potatoes, sliced to a thickness of 1 cm/½ inch

salt

For the masala (curry paste)

6 fresh green chillies

6 garlic cloves, peeled

2 green cardamom pods

2.5 cm/1 inch piece of fresh ginger, peeled

2 tablespoons red wine vinegar

2 cloves

1 teaspoon sugar

½ teaspoon cumin seeds

½ teaspoon turmeric powder

juice of ½ lime

1 large bunch of fresh coriander leaves

Serves 4–6

Pierce the poussins all over with a fork, place in a dish and sprinkle over the lime juice and some salt. Put in the fridge for about 30 minutes.

Meanwhile, put all the masala ingredients into a food processor and whiz to form a green paste.

Spread the paste all over the poussins and leave to marinate again in the fridge for about 2 hours.

Heat some vegetable oil in a large pan, add the poussins and fry, turning frequently, until they are brown and crispy – about 20 minutes, or until the meat is cooked.

Remove the poussins from the pan and set aside to keep warm, leaving the cooking juices in the pan.

Fry the potato slices in the remaining juices until they are golden brown on both sides and serve hot with the poussins.

Duck and ginger go very well together. Because it is so fatty, duck retains its flavour through the cooking process; this is a lovely, slightly unusual dish.

Frogs' legs are widely used in Vietnam and, if you are able to obtain them, this recipe makes an interesting change from the French method of cooking them. However, should you feel unable to take this route, chicken wings will work very well.

Curried Duck with Ginger

Frogs' Legs, Vietnamese Style

4 duck joints, skin and fat left on

2 red onions, peeled and thinly sliced

4 cm/1½ inch piece of fresh ginger, peeled and cut into fine strips

8–10 garlic cloves, peeled and crushed

2 fresh red chillies, deseeded and cut into fine strips

1 kg/2¼ lb tomatoes, skinned and deseeded

salt and freshly ground black pepper

Serves 4–6

Put the duck joints in a large pan and cover with water. Bring to the boil, then simmer, uncovered, for about 1 hour until the water has evaporated and the duck is cooked and sitting in its own fat. Strain off the fat and cover the duck joints with a little more water.

Add the remaining ingredients and simmer for 25–30 minutes until the duck is coated in a thick sauce. Season and serve.

450 g/1 lb large frogs' legs

1 small onion, peeled and finely chopped

vegetable oil, for frying

200 ml/7 fl oz coconut milk

225 ml/8 fl oz chicken stock

salt and freshly ground black pepper

fresh coriander leaves, to garnish

For the masala (curry paste)

2 shallots, peeled and finely diced

2 garlic cloves, peeled and finely diced

2 or 3 fresh red chillies, coarsely chopped

1 stalk of lemon grass, finely chopped

1 tablespoon curry powder

1 heaped teaspoon brown sugar

a dash of fish sauce

Serves 4–6

Blend all the ingredients for the masala in a food processor until smooth. Cover the frogs' legs with the paste and put to one side.

Sauté the onion in a little vegetable oil until soft, then add the coated frogs' legs and sauté for 2–3 minutes on each side. Season with salt and pepper.

Stir in the coconut milk and simmer gently for about 15 minutes. If it becomes too dry, add a little chicken stock to achieve a smooth sauce.

Garnish with the coriander leaves and serve with rice or noodles.

Meat Curries

This classic Asian dish makes a great change from good old beef casserole. It is quite hot and dry, but the addition of the coconut milk softens this. It is very delicious served with plain boiled rice.

Beef Rendang

1.5 kg/3 lb 5 oz braising steak, cut into 2.5 cm/ 1 inch cubes

6 dried red chillies, crushed

1 stalk of lemon grass, crushed

6 shallots, peeled and finely chopped

3 garlic cloves, peeled and finely chopped

vegetable oil, for frying

1 tablespoon turmeric powder

5–6 Kaffir lime leaves

½ teaspoon tamarind concentrate

juice of 2 limes

a 400 ml/14 fl oz tin of coconut milk

salt and freshly ground black pepper

Serves 4–6

Put the chillies, lemon grass, shallots and garlic into a food processor and whiz to form a paste.

Heat some vegetable oil in a large casserole and brown the beef. Remove the beef and set aside.

Using the same casserole, fry the paste, stirring all the time, for about 1 minute. Add the turmeric, lime leaves, tamarind concentrate, lime juice and some black pepper and mix well.

Add the beef and the coconut milk, cover the pan and cook gently for about 1 hour until the beef is cooked and quite dry. Add salt to taste and serve.

The meatballs are cooked twice – first to brown them all over and then they are simmered in the curry sauce.

The people of Goa add vinegar to lots of their dishes, giving them a distinctive flavour. This is a fairly hot dish – adjust the chillies to your taste.

Curried Meatballs

450 g/1 lb lean minced beef

2 onions, peeled and finely chopped

4 garlic cloves, peeled and finely chopped

2 teaspoons coriander powder

2 teaspoons chilli powder

2 teaspoons turmeric powder

1 teaspoon cumin powder

1 teaspoon ground ginger

1 egg, beaten

vegetable oil, for frying

ghee or clarified butter

salt

a good handful of fresh coriander leaves, chopped, to garnish

Serves 4–6

Put the beef, half each of the onions, garlic and spices into a large bowl, add salt to taste, then mix together. Bind the mixture with the beaten egg.

Using your hands, form small meatballs from the beef mixture.

Heat about 2.5–5 cm/1–2 inches of vegetable oil in a pan and gently deep-fry the meatballs for about 5 minutes. Remove from the pan and drain on kitchen paper.

Heat the ghee or clarified butter in a separate pan and stir-fry the remaining onion and garlic until they have softened, then stir in the remaining spices. Season and stir-fry for 3–4 minutes.

Add the meatballs to this mixture, stirring them around to coat them with the mixture, then add 200 ml/7 fl oz of water, bring to the boil and simmer over a low heat for about 30 minutes.

Serve garnished with the chopped coriander.

Goan Beef Curry

1 kg/2¼ lb stewing or braising beef, cut into 2.5 cm/ 1 inch cubes

vegetable oil, for frying

2 red onions, peeled and finely chopped

2 tomatoes, skinned, deseeded and finely chopped

4 fresh green chillies, finely chopped

2 tablespoons finely chopped fresh coriander leaves

4 dried red chillies

10 peppercorns, finely ground in 1 tablespoon vinegar

2.5 cm/1 inch piece of fresh ginger, peeled and grated

½ teaspoon cumin seeds

½ teaspoon turmeric powder

salt

Serves 4–6

Heat some vegetable oil in a large frying pan and stir-fry the onions, tomatoes, green chillies and coriander leaves for 5 minutes.

Add the red chillies, peppercorn mixture, ginger, cumin seeds and turmeric powder and stir-fry for about 2 minutes.

Add the meat and stir until it is browned, then add about 1 cup of water, cover the pan and cook until the meat is tender – about 30 minutes. Season to taste with salt and serve with rice.

Everyone loves roast beef and this makes a wonderful change from
the norm.

Spiced Roast Beef

2 kg/4½ lb sirloin
of beef

2.5 cm/1 inch piece
of fresh ginger, peeled

8 garlic cloves, peeled

1 tablespoon
lemon juice

vegetable oil, for
frying

10 peppercorns

1 cinnamon stick

8 cloves

6 dried red chillies

1 tablespoon
Worcestershire sauce

1 dessertspoon
cornflour

salt

Serves 4–6

Grind the ginger and garlic together to make a fine paste. Pat the meat
dry with kitchen paper, prick with a fork and rub in the ginger/garlic
paste, lemon juice and salt to taste. Marinate in the fridge for about
6 hours, turning regularly.

Preheat the oven to 190°C/375°F/mark 5. Heat a little vegetable oil in
a large oven dish and brown the meat all over. Add 1 cup of water, the
peppercorns, cinnamon, cloves and chillies and roast in the oven for
about 2–2½ hours until cooked. Remove the meat and put aside
to rest.

Mix the Worcestershire sauce with a little water and the cornflour and
stir into the pan juices. Stir over a low heat until thickened.

Slice the beef, arrange on a serving dish, then pour the sauce over
and serve.

To make tamarind water cover some tamarind pulp with water, bring to the boil and leave to cool. Squeeze out the tamarind and use the water as needed.

Hot-chillied Indonesian Steak

575 g/1 lb 5 oz rump steak, chilled in the fridge

2 teaspoons coriander powder

2 tablespoons tamarind water

1 teaspoon brown sugar

8 fresh red chillies, deseeded and finely chopped

4 shallots, peeled and finely chopped

2 garlic cloves, peeled and finely chopped

vegetable oil, for frying

1 teaspoon lemon juice

salt and freshly ground black pepper

Serves 4–6

Using a sharp knife, slice the meat very thinly across the grain and then cut the slices into 5 cm/2 inch squares. Put in a dish in a single layer and sprinkle with the coriander, tamarind water and sugar and season to taste with salt and pepper. Press the spices down well and leave to marinate in the fridge for about 2 hours.

Put the chillies, shallots and garlic into a food processor and whiz quickly until fine, but not quite a paste.

Heat some vegetable oil in a pan and fry the meat until browned and cooked through. Using a slotted spoon, remove the meat from the pan and keep it warm.

Add the chilli mixture to the remaining oil in the pan and fry, stirring well, for a couple of minutes.

Return the meat to the pan and stir well to coat the meat. Add the lemon juice and serve hot with rice.

This is a hot curry, with a marvellous mix of flavours in it that work brilliantly together. Best to serve this with a sweet chutney, such as mango (see page 136), and a little natural yoghurt.

Hot Drunken Beef

700 g/1½ lb lean beef, such as sirloin steaks, sliced into thin strips

2 shallots, peeled and finely chopped

2.5 cm/1 inch piece of fresh ginger, peeled and finely chopped

2 garlic cloves, peeled and finely chopped

2 fresh bird's eye chillies, finely chopped

1 fresh red chilli, deseeded and sliced lengthways

1 fresh green chilli, deseeded and sliced lengthways

vegetable oil, for frying

1 teaspoon green peppercorns

4 Kaffir lime leaves, shredded

100 g/3½ oz fine green beans, cut into 2.5 cm/1 inch lengths

1 tablespoon fish sauce

1 teaspoon soft brown sugar

2 teaspoons red wine vinegar

whisky, to flame

a small handful of fresh basil leaves, to garnish

Serves 4–6

Put the shallots, ginger, garlic and all the chillies into a food processor and whiz to a paste.

Heat a little vegetable oil in a frying pan and fry this mixture for about 1 minute, then add the beef, peppercorns, lime leaves and green beans and fry for about 5 minutes.

Add the fish sauce, brown sugar and vinegar and stir well for about 2 minutes.

Pour in the whisky and set alight to flame the dish. When the flames have gone out, garnish with the basil leaves and serve.

The coconut milk provides a rich creamy sauce typical of many Thai dishes, and is spiced up by the familiar ingredients that go to make up the curry paste.

Hot Thai Beef Curry

450 g/1 lb braising steak, sliced thinly and cut into strips

2 tablespoons yellow bean sauce

2 tablespoons Thai red curry paste

4 fresh green chillies, deseeded and finely chopped

4 garlic cloves, peeled and finely chopped

3 shallots, peeled and finely chopped

1 stalk of lemon grass, finely chopped

2.5 cm/1 inch piece of fresh ginger, peeled and grated

1 teaspoon shrimp paste

juice of 1 lime

2 tablespoons caster sugar

a 400 ml/14 fl oz tin of coconut milk

Serves 4–6

Put all the ingredients except the steak and coconut milk into a food processor and whiz to a paste.

Put the beef and coconut milk in a large pan and bring to the boil. Cover and simmer for about 40 minutes.

Add the spicy paste and mix thoroughly, then cover and cook for another 10 minutes.

Serve with your favourite rice (see pages 128–132).

Vindaloo tends to make one think of those dark, hot things that lurk in Indian takeaways. An authentic Vindaloo, however, is nothing like that. Gently red in colour and brimming with flavour rather than heat, it is a joy.

You can make this dish using just pork, but if you can find fresh eel, do have a go with it. It is delicious.

Pork Vindaloo

800 g/1¾ lb pork, diced	Put all the masala ingredients except the vinegar into a food processor and whiz, then add the vinegar to make a smooth paste.
vegetable oil for frying	
2 red onions, peeled and finely chopped	
4 potatoes, peeled and cut into 2.5 cm/1 inch cubes	Heat some vegetable oil in a pan and fry the onions until they are soft, then add the masala and stir-fry for a couple of minutes.
sugar	
salt	

Stir in the pork and cook for a couple of minutes, or until the ingredients are all mixed. Add a little water to make a thickish sauce and simmer gently until the meat is nearly cooked.

For the masala (curry paste)

13–15 dried red chillies

4 fresh green chillies

2.5 cm/1 inch piece of fresh ginger, peeled

2 cinnamon sticks

4 cloves

1 teaspoon cumin seeds

1 teaspoon black peppercorns

1 teaspoon turmeric powder

100 ml/3½ fl oz red wine vinegar

Add the potatoes, a little sugar and salt to taste and continue cooking until the potatoes are cooked.

Serve with the rice of your choice (see pages 128–132).

Serves 4–6

Pork and Eel Curry with Red Salad

1 kg/2¼ lb shoulder of pork, cubed

700 g/1½ lb eel, skinned, boned and cut into pieces

vegetable oil, for frying

2 red onions, peeled and thinly sliced

700 g/1½ lb tomatoes, skinned, deseeded and finely chopped

8 garlic cloves, peeled and crushed

2 fresh red chillies, finely chopped

2.5 cm/1 inch piece of fresh ginger, peeled and grated

salt

For the red salad

1 red onion, peeled and finely chopped

6 spring onions, chopped

3 fresh plum tomatoes, skinned, deseeded and finely chopped

juice of ½ lime

salt

Prepare the red salad by mixing the onions and tomatoes together, then sprinkle over the lime juice and season with salt. Put in the fridge.

Heat a little vegetable oil in a large saucepan and fry the pork to seal it without colouring it. Cover with water and simmer for 50 minutes until tender.

Sprinkle the pieces of eel with salt and add to the pan with the onions, tomatoes, garlic, chillies and ginger. Simmer, uncovered, for about 20 minutes.

Serve with the red salad.

Serves 4–6

This is a very substantial, peasant-type dish that is highly spiced, but
the addition of offal does make it very flavoursome.

Goan Sorpotel

1 kg/2¼ lb boneless
pork (leg or shoulder)

1 pig's liver

1 pig's heart

2 pig's kidneys

10 black peppercorns

1 teaspoon
cumin seeds

8 cloves

2 cinnamon sticks

12 dried red chillies

10 garlic
cloves, peeled

2.5 cm/1 inch piece
of fresh ginger, peeled

150 ml/¼ pint red
wine vinegar

vegetable oil, for
frying

4 red onions, peeled
and finely chopped

6 fresh green chillies,
deseeded and
finely chopped

salt

Serves 4–6

Put all the meats in a large pan, cover with water and simmer for about
20 minutes until partially cooked. Remove from the pan and dice finely.
Reserve the cooking liquid.

Put all the spices and the dried red chillies, garlic, ginger and vinegar
into a food processor and whiz until you have a fine paste.

Heat some vegetable oil in a large pan and gently fry all the meat,
stirring continuously, until lightly browned.

Add to this the spice paste and salt to taste and stir-fry for 5 minutes,
then add the reserved meat stock, chopped onions and green chillies.

Lower the heat, cover the pan and simmer for 45 minutes–1 hour,
stirring occasionally, until the sauce has thickened and the oils have
risen to the top.

This dish can be served with poppadoms or naan bread and the taste
improves if it is left overnight and reheated.

Pork really takes up the flavour of any marinade, in this case soy sauce and pepper. Here, it's then simmered with ginger, onion and garlic to provide a mildly spiced curry.

Golden Pork

1 kg/2¼ lb shoulder or leg of pork, cut into bite-sized pieces

3 tablespoons soy sauce

4 cm/1½ inch piece of fresh ginger, peeled – purée half of this, cut the other half into fine strips

2 onions, peeled and puréed

3 garlic cloves, peeled and crushed

1 teaspoon chilli powder

vegetable oil, for frying

freshly ground black pepper

Serves 4–6

Put the pork into a bowl with 2 tablespoons of the soy sauce and plenty of black pepper and leave to marinate for 2 hours in the fridge, or 1 hour at room temperature.

Put the puréed ginger, the onions and garlic into a bowl and pour over a little boiling water. Stir, then strain off and reserve the flavoured water and put both to one side.

Stir the chilli powder into a little boiling water.

Heat some vegetable oil in a large frying pan and quickly stir-fry the strips of ginger, then add the pork and stir-fry until the pork is golden brown.

Add the flavoured water and simmer, covered, for about 10 minutes until all the liquid is absorbed.

Add the remaining soy sauce, the chilli water and the ginger, onion and garlic purée. Cover the pan and cook gently for about 40 minutes, adding a little water if necessary, until the pork is tender.

This is really just a variation on standard meat loaf, but the addition of the fish sauce and chillies really does make a plain dish a little unusual.

Vietnamese Meat Loaf

500 g/1 lb 2 oz minced pork	Preheat the oven to 190°C/375°F/mark 5. Put all the ingredients except the eggs into a large mixing bowl and mix very well together.
500 g/1 lb 2 oz minced pig's liver	Make a well in the middle of the mixture and break in 3 of the eggs, then, using your hands, thoroughly combine the eggs with the pork mixture.
50 g/2 oz field mushrooms, finely chopped	
3 garlic cloves, peeled and finely chopped	Pack the mixture into a 900 g/2 lb loaf tin, pressing down well. Beat the remaining egg and brush it over the top of the loaf.

500 g/1 lb 2 oz
minced pork

500 g/1 lb 2 oz
minced pig's liver

50 g/2 oz field
mushrooms,
finely chopped

3 garlic cloves, peeled
and finely chopped

4 shallots, peeled and
finely chopped

50 g/2 oz tinned
anchovy fillets in oil,
finely chopped

1 tablespoon
fish sauce

2 fresh red chillies,
deseeded and
finely chopped

freshly ground
black pepper

4 eggs

Serves 4–6

Preheat the oven to 190°C/375°F/mark 5. Put all the ingredients except the eggs into a large mixing bowl and mix very well together.

Make a well in the middle of the mixture and break in 3 of the eggs, then, using your hands, thoroughly combine the eggs with the pork mixture.

Pack the mixture into a 900 g/2 lb loaf tin, pressing down well. Beat the remaining egg and brush it over the top of the loaf.

Place the loaf tin in a roasting tin of water, so that the water comes about halfway up the sides of the loaf tin, and cover the whole roasting tin with foil. Cook in the oven for about 45 minutes. The loaf is cooked when you prick with a knife and the juices run clear.

Remove from the oven, cool slightly and turn out onto a plate.

This dish can be served hot or cold.

The sesame and peanut oils add a lovely flavour to this dish while the turmeric provides colour.

Burmese-style Pork

1.5 kg/3 lb 5 oz pork, cubed

1 red onion, peeled

12 garlic cloves, peeled

1 cm/½ inch piece of fresh ginger, peeled

8 shallots, peeled

2 tablespoons white wine vinegar

1 tablespoon sesame oil

3 tablespoons peanut oil

2 fresh red chillies, finely chopped

1 teaspoon turmeric powder

1 teaspoon shrimp paste

Serves 4–6

Put the onion, garlic, ginger, shallots and vinegar into a food processor and whiz together. Transfer to a bowl and mix in the pork. Leave to marinate in the fridge for about 2 hours.

When the pork has marinated, take out the meat, reserving the marinade. Heat the sesame oil and 2 tablespoons of the peanut oil in a large pan and fry the pork, turning until lightly golden all over. Cover with water, bring to the boil and simmer for 1½ hours.

In another pan, heat the remaining peanut oil, add the marinade mixture and the chillies and fry for 4–5 minutes. Add the turmeric and shrimp paste and fry for a couple more minutes.

Add this to the cooked pork mixture, stirring well, and simmer for a further 10 minutes.

Tasty dish - perhaps try chicken

The combination of pork and aubergines works very well. When preparing the aubergines, lay the uncooked cubes in a sieve and sprinkle with salt. Leave for about 10 minutes and you will see they release a lot of liquid. Pat them dry, then fry them. They will keep their texture and flavour better if you do this. The addition of sherry to this dish gives it a distinctly Chinese flavour.

Pork and Aubergines with Chillies

200 g/7 oz lean pork, cubed	Put the pork, ginger, garlic, soy sauce and sherry into a large bowl, mix together and leave in the fridge for 30 minutes.
1 cm/½ inch piece of fresh ginger, peeled and grated	
2 garlic cloves, peeled and chopped	Heat some vegetable oil in a heavy-bottomed pan and fry the aubergine until golden. Remove and drain on kitchen paper.
1 tablespoon soy sauce	
1 teaspoon dry sherry	
vegetable oil, for frying	In the same pan, fry the pork mixture, turning frequently, for about 2 minutes, then add the aubergine and chillies and cook for a further 2 minutes.
225 g/8 oz aubergine, cubed (see above)	
2 fresh red chillies, finely chopped	
4 tablespoons chicken stock	Add the stock, cover and cook until nearly all the liquid has gone. Add salt to taste and serve hot, garnished with the chopped spring onions.
salt	
2 spring onions, finely chopped, to garnish	

Serves 4–6

Another great snack food. They can be eaten hot or cold. If you serve them as a main course, make the balls a little larger.

Pork Balls with Lemon Grass

450 g/1 lb lean minced pork	Put all the ingredients except the vegetable oil into a large bowl and mix together. Then, using your hands, form the mixture into small balls.
4 stalks of lemon grass, very finely chopped	
1 cm/½ inch piece of fresh ginger, peeled and grated	Fry the pork balls in about 2.5 cm/ 1 inch of hot oil for 4–5 minutes until golden brown. Remove with a slotted spoon and drain on kitchen paper.
2 tomatoes, skinned, deseeded and finely chopped	
1 teaspoon turmeric powder	Serve by themselves as a snack or with rice.
juice of ½ lime	
2 tablespoons Thai red curry paste	
vegetable oil, for frying	

Serves 4–6

This is a one-pot dish that just needs rice and a relish to accompany it. You could also make it with chicken instead of lamb. This recipe will need to be started the day before.

Lamb Dhansak

500 g/1 lb 2 oz stewing lamb or mutton, cut into cubes

500 g/1 lb 2 oz yellow lentils

110 g/4 oz red lentils

110 g/4 oz mung peas, soaked overnight

oil or ghee, for frying

2 red onions, peeled and finely sliced

½ teaspoon turmeric powder

1 teaspoon coriander powder

1 teaspoon cumin powder

1 aubergine, peeled and diced

250 g/9 oz pumpkin, peeled and diced

salt

500 g/1 lb 2 oz fresh spinach leaves, well washed and drained

For the masala (curry paste)

6–8 garlic cloves, peeled

5 cm/2 inch piece of fresh ginger, peeled and chopped

6–8 dried red chillies

6 green cardamom pods

1 cinnamon stick

½ teaspoon black peppercorns

1 tablespoon coriander seeds

1 tablespoon cumin seeds

Serves 4–6

Rinse and drain the lentils and mung peas. Grind all the masala ingredients with a little water to make a smooth paste.

Heat the oil or ghee and fry the onions until golden brown, then stir in the masala paste, turmeric, coriander and cumin and stir-fry gently for about 5 minutes.

Stir in the lamb and cook gently over a low heat until the meat is coated with the masala paste and any liquid from the meat has been absorbed. The dish should be quite dry.

Add the lentils, peas, aubergine and pumpkin and stir in a little water to form a gravy. Season with salt. Bring to the boil, then reduce the heat, cover and simmer gently for about 30 minutes until the meat is cooked.

Remove the meat from the pan and put to one side. Purée the lentils, vegetables and gravy in a food processor and return the meat to this mixture.

Quickly stir-fry the spinach in hot oil, then add to the lamb mixture and serve.

This may sound a little strange, but in fact cooking in milk is commonplace in parts of Asia and makes for a nice, subtle, pale curry.

Kashmiri Lamb in Milk

750 g/1 lb 10 oz lamb chops

250 g/9 oz lamb bones, for stock

a pinch of saffron

vegetable oil, for frying

2 red onions, peeled and finely grated

2 cloves

2 cinnamon sticks

5 green cardamom pods

1.2 litres/2 pints milk

2 tablespoons single cream

1 teaspoon fennel powder

½ teaspoon cumin powder

½ teaspoon ground white pepper

½ teaspoon sugar

1 fresh green chilli, deseeded and finely sliced

salt and freshly ground black pepper

Soak the saffron in 2 tablespoons of water.

Heat a little vegetable oil in a pan and fry the onions until soft and golden.

Put the lamb chops and bones in a large pan with about 600 ml/1 pint of water, 1 clove, 1 cinnamon stick, 3 cardamom pods, the onions and a pinch of salt. Bring to the boil, then cover the pan and simmer for about 15–20 minutes until the meat is tender. Strain and reserve the stock, keeping the chops but discarding the bones.

Pour the milk into another saucepan and add the remaining clove, cinnamon stick and cardamom pods. Bring to the boil, stirring gently, and cook until the milk reduces by about a third. Take off the heat and strain, then pour back into the pan. Set aside until cool, then stir in the cream.

Add the chops and about 300 ml/½ pint of the stock to the spiced milk and warm over a low heat.

Heat a little more oil in a frying pan and add the fennel and cumin powders and the white pepper and fry for a few seconds. Add this to the chops and stock mixture, and stir in the sugar. Season to taste.

Add the chilli and the saffron to the lamb mixture and simmer for 2–3 minutes, then serve with rice.

Serves 4–6

The coriander-flavoured yoghurt tenderises this lamb dish and lying
in wait for the unwary are whole green chillies stuffed with a fennel,
mustard, cumin and fenugreek mixture.

Pickling-spiced Lamb

800 g/1¾ lb shoulder
or leg of lamb, cut
into bite-sized pieces

2 good handfuls of
fresh coriander leaves

270 ml/9 fl oz natural
yoghurt

2 red onions, peeled
and chopped

2 garlic cloves, peeled

2.5 cm/1 inch piece
of fresh ginger, peeled

1 heaped teaspoon
fennel seeds

1 teaspoon
mustard seeds

1 teaspoon
cumin seeds

1 teaspoon
fenugreek seeds

8 fresh green chillies

vegetable oil, for
frying

½ teaspoon
turmeric powder

salt

Serves 4–6

Put the coriander leaves and yoghurt into a food processor and whiz
together. Tip into a bowl and set aside.

Put the onions, garlic and ginger into the food processor and whiz
together, then set aside.

Grind together the fennel, mustard, cumin and fenugreek seeds. Slit the
green chillies down one side and remove the seeds to create a pocket,
then stuff the pocket with half of the spice mixture. Reserve the rest.

Heat some vegetable oil in a large pan and fry the stuffed chillies for a
couple of minutes. Add the puréed onion mixture and cook gently for
about 10 minutes.

Add the reserved spices and stir for about 1 minute, then add the
yoghurt mix, turmeric powder and some salt. Bring to the boil, add the
meat and mix well.

Turn down the heat, cover the pan and simmer until the meat is tender,
45 minutes–1 hour.

Serve with Saffron Rice with Cumin (see page 131).

Lamb chops are coated in a creamy marinade and left for about 5 hours at room temperature, longer if they are in the fridge. You could serve these with a vegetable curry and rice.

This dish is quite dry when cooked, but it is full of flavour. Served in pitta bread with yoghurt, it makes a great snack meal.

Spicy Lamb Chops

Curried Lamb with Coriander

8 thick lamb chops, trimmed of fat

a good handful of unsalted cashew nuts

450 ml/¾ pint milk

a little vegetable oil

2 teaspoons ground white pepper

3 garlic cloves, peeled

2.5 cm/1 inch piece of fresh ginger, peeled

450 ml/¾ pint natural yoghurt

4 fresh green chillies, finely chopped

2 teaspoons mixed mace, nutmeg and cardamom powder

1 teaspoon ground ginger

salt

Serves 4–6

Soak the cashew nuts in the milk for about 30 minutes, then drain and liquidise to form a paste. Set this aside.

Meanwhile, place the chops in an ovenproof dish and rub with vegetable oil, the white pepper and some salt and put in the fridge for 10–15 minutes. Grind the garlic and ginger together into a paste.

Put the yoghurt, cashew nut paste, chillies, ginger and garlic paste, mixed mace, nutmeg and cardamom powder, ground ginger and salt into a food processor and whiz until you have a creamy marinade.

Pour over the chops and leave aside for about 5 hours, longer if you put them in the fridge.

Preheat the oven to 220°C/425°F/ mark 7. Place the chops on a trivet in a roasting tray and roast in the oven for 10 minutes, then turn and roast for another 10 minutes.

Finally, finish the chops off under a hot grill for a couple of minutes on both sides to fully brown them.

750 g/1 lb 10 oz minced lamb

vegetable oil, for frying

2 medium red onions, peeled and finely chopped

5 garlic cloves, peeled and finely chopped

1 cm/½ inch piece of fresh ginger, peeled and grated

2 fresh green chillies, finely chopped

3 cloves

3 green cardamom pods, crushed

¼ teaspoon turmeric powder

1½ teaspoons coriander powder

1 teaspoon cumin powder

1 teaspoon garam masala powder

2 tomatoes, finely chopped

1 cinnamon stick

a good handful of chopped fresh coriander leaves

salt

Heat a little vegetable oil in a pan and fry the onions until they are golden.

Add the garlic, ginger and chillies and cook for a couple of minutes, then add the lamb and fry for about 5 minutes.

Add the cloves, cardamom pods, turmeric, coriander, cumin and half the garam masala powders and cook, stirring, for another few minutes. Add the tomatoes and cinnamon stick and season to taste.

When the tomatoes are cooked, add a couple of cups of water and continue to cook for about 30 minutes until the lamb is cooked and tender.

Add the chopped coriander and remaining garam masala and cook for a few more minutes until you have a fairly dry consistency.

Serve with pitta bread and natural yoghurt.

Serves 4–6

Ground almonds enrich this smooth gravy, in which is simmered lamb or mutton. You can buy rosewater in most chemist stores.

Rogan Josh

800 g/1¾ lb lamb or mutton, cut into bite-sized pieces

225 ml/8 fl oz natural yoghurt

100 g/3½ oz tomato purée

1 tablespoon ground almonds

salt

For the masala (curry paste)

vegetable oil, for frying

4 cardamom pods

4 cloves

4 tablespoons ginger and garlic purée (just take equal quantities of peeled garlic and fresh ginger and purée together)

1 teaspoon chilli powder

2 tablespoons brown onion paste (sauté finely diced red onions in oil until golden brown, then purée)

½ tablespoon garam masala powder

For the garnish

chopped fresh coriander leaves

2.5 cm/1 inch piece of fresh ginger, peeled and cut into thin strips

a good pinch of saffron threads, soaked in 3 tablespoons rosewater

Serves 4–6

To make the masala, heat some oil, add the cardamom pods and cloves and fry until they crackle. Add the rest of the masala ingredients and stir-fry for a minute or so.

Stir in the lamb and yoghurt, season with salt and stir-fry for 3–4 minutes to coat the lamb with the yoghurt and masala. Add a little water and simmer gently for about 45 minutes to 1 hour until the lamb is almost tender.

Mix in the tomato purée and continue cooking until the liquid is reduced by about one-third. Stir in the ground almonds.

Turn out into a serving dish, garnish with the coriander leaves and ginger strips, sprinkle on the saffron and rosewater and serve.

This must be cooked in a very hot oven to achieve that authentic tandoori appearance and flavour. The addition of melted butter at the end gives it additional richness.

Tandoori Lamb

4 small racks of lamb

2 tablespoons melted butter

For the marinade

300 ml/½ pint natural yoghurt

3 tablespoons double cream

1 egg yolk

6 garlic cloves, peeled and finely chopped

2.5 cm/1 inch piece of fresh ginger, peeled and grated

juice of 1 lime

2 teaspoons chilli powder

2 teaspoons garam masala powder

1 teaspoon turmeric powder

a small handful of fresh coriander leaves

1 teaspoon freshly ground black pepper

salt

Serves 4–6

To make the marinade, mix together the yoghurt, cream and egg yolk in a small bowl.

Put the garlic, ginger, lime juice and some salt into a food processor, whiz together, then stir into the yoghurt mixture. Add all the other marinade ingredients and stir well.

Remove any skin from the lamb and prick holes all over the meat. Rub the marinade well into the lamb, cover and leave in the fridge, preferably overnight.

Preheat the oven to 220°C/425°F/mark 7. Roast the lamb in the oven for 20–25 minutes, or longer if you do not like your meat too rare.

When the lamb is cooked, remove from the oven and brush all over with the melted butter, then return to the oven for 2–3 minutes more.

Slice and serve with a salad.

Marinated lamb is served in a creamy, aromatic sauce. Try it with
Saffron Rice with Cumin (see page 131).

Lamb in Spiced Sauce

500 g/1 lb 2 oz lamb, cut into bite-sized pieces

2.5 cm/1 inch piece of fresh ginger, peeled and grated

3 garlic cloves, peeled and crushed

vegetable oil, for frying

2 blades mace

10 green cardamom pods

4 black cardamom pods

10 cloves

3 bay leaves

2 red onions, peeled and finely diced

½ teaspoon turmeric powder

½ teaspoon chilli powder

1 teaspoon coriander powder

150 ml/¼ pint tomato purée

50 ml/2 fl oz double cream

salt

Purée together the ginger and garlic and use half of it to spread on the lamb, then leave for 1 hour for the flavours to infuse.

Heat some vegetable oil in a pan and fry the mace, green and black cardamom pods, cloves and bay leaves until they crackle, then add the onions and stir-fry until they are golden brown.

Add the rest of the garlic and ginger paste and all the other spices, season with salt and cook for a few minutes.

Stir in the lamb and cook until sealed, then add a little water, cover the pan and simmer the lamb for about 45 minutes to 1 hour until tender.

When the lamb is cooked, remove from the juices and set aside. Pour the sauce into a food processor and whiz until smooth. Strain it into another pan and gently reheat, then add the tomato purée and simmer until it is rich and thick. Lower the heat and stir in the cream, then season and place the lamb in the sauce to reheat. Serve hot.

Serves 4–6

This is a dish for a special occasion. Succulent lamb is combined with fragrant rice and decorated with nuts, herbs and ghee.

Lamb Biryani

2 kg/4½ lb lamb, cut into bite-sized pieces

4 garlic cloves, peeled

2.5 cm/1 inch piece of fresh ginger, peeled

2 teaspoons chilli powder

1 kg/2¼ lb basmati rice, thoroughly washed in cold water, drained and soaked in fresh water for 1 hour

ghee or clarified butter

2 red onions, peeled and finely chopped

100 g/3½ oz flaked almonds

270 ml/9 fl oz natural yoghurt

100 ml/3½ fl oz double cream

100 g/3½ oz sultanas

100 g/3½ oz cashew nuts

a large handful of fresh mint leaves, chopped

a large handful of fresh coriander leaves, chopped

a few drops of rosewater (see page 61)

a pinch of saffron threads, soaked in 2 tablespoons water

juice of 1 large lemon

salt

For the masala (curry paste)

10 cardamom pods

10 cloves

4 blades mace

1 teaspoon cinnamon powder

Serves 4–6

Roast the spices for the masala in a dry pan for a few seconds, then grind them and put to one side.

Purée the garlic and ginger together and mix in the chilli powder.

Heat some ghee in a large pan and stir-fry the onions until they are soft and slightly browned, then stir in the masala powder and the garlic and ginger purée and cook for about 5 minutes, stirring all the time.

Stir in half the flaked almonds and add the lamb, then stir in the yoghurt and a little water, cover the pan and cook for about 1 hour until the lamb is tender.

Meanwhile, drain the rice thoroughly. Heat some ghee or clarified butter in a large frying pan and sauté the rice for about 3 minutes, making sure all the grains are coated in the fat.

Add enough water to just cover the rice, season and cook gently over a low heat until the rice is cooked and the water has evaporated. Set aside and keep the rice warm.

Stir the cream into the lamb and continue to cook gently to warm through. Sprinkle in half the sultanas, half the cashew nuts and half the chopped herbs and pour the lamb into a serving dish.

Mix the rest of the sultanas, cashew nuts, herbs and the rosewater, saffron and lemon juice with the rice and spoon the rice evenly over the lamb.

Toast the remaining flaked almonds in a dry pan and sprinkle them over the dish along with some melted ghee.

This is a substantial curry, needing little more than some naan bread (see page 133). You can ask your butcher to chop up the lamb for you.

The vinegar, sugar and apricots give this curry a slightly sweet piquancy. If you're short of time you could use no-soak, soft, dried apricots.

Curried Lamb with Green Peas

Lamb Curry with Apricots

1 kg/2¼ lb lamb shank, cut into steaks across the bone

vegetable oil, for frying

3 onions, peeled and finely chopped

1 tablespoon red masala curry paste

1 star anise

5 fresh green chillies, chopped

5 garlic cloves, peeled and finely chopped

a few sprigs of fresh thyme

1 litre/1¾ pints chicken or lamb stock

450 g/1 lb potatoes, cut into small cubes

450 g/1 lb frozen peas

salt and freshly ground black pepper

Serves 4–6

Heat some vegetable oil in a large frying pan and brown the lamb steaks.

Add the onions and cook until they are softened, then add the curry paste, star anise, chillies, garlic and thyme.

Pour in the stock, cover and cook for 20 minutes.

Add the potatoes and cook for another 20 minutes or until the potatoes are cooked.

Add the peas, bring back to a simmer and cook for 5–10 minutes, then season to taste and serve.

750 g/1 lb 10 oz stewing lamb, cut into bite-sized pieces

vegetable oil, for frying

2 red onions, peeled and very finely chopped

1 cm/½ inch piece of fresh ginger, peeled and grated

4 garlic cloves, peeled and crushed

1 cinnamon stick

4 green cardamom pods, lightly crushed

1½ teaspoons chilli powder

2 teaspoons cumin powder

3 tomatoes, skinned, deseeded and finely chopped

¾ teaspoon garam masala powder

1 teaspoon red wine vinegar

1 teaspoon sugar

100 g/3½ oz dried apricots, soaked in water for 3 hours to soften

salt and freshly ground black pepper

Heat some vegetable oil in a large frying pan and stir-fry the onions until they are golden.

Add the ginger and garlic and cook for a couple more minutes.

Add the cinnamon stick and cardamom pods, cook for a minute, then add the chilli and cumin powders and stir well to amalgamate.

Add the tomatoes and cook for 5–6 minutes, then add the meat, garam masala and black pepper to taste and stir-fry for 5–7 minutes.

Season with salt, cover the pan and cook slowly over a low heat for about 45 minutes to 1 hour until tender.

At the last minute stir in the vinegar, sugar and apricots and heat through, stirring well.

Serves 4–6

Fish Curries

Amazingly, carrots and prawns do go together. With the lemon grass, mint, chillies, lemon juice and lime leaves, this soup is very light and very quick to make.

Spicy Carrot and Prawn Soup

500 ml/18 fl oz fresh carrot juice

12 large raw prawns, peeled and deveined (see page 72)

1 tablespoon finely chopped lemon grass

2 or 3 fresh red chillies, finely chopped

4 or 5 fresh or dried Kaffir lime leaves, finely chopped

1 small bunch of fresh coriander leaves, finely chopped

1 small bunch of fresh mint leaves, finely chopped

a dash of fish sauce

juice of 1 lime or 1 lemon

salt and freshly ground black pepper

110 g/4 oz butter, melted, to serve

chopped fresh coriander leaves, to garnish

Serves 4–6

Heat the carrot juice in a pan with the lemon grass, chillies, lime leaves, coriander and mint and simmer gently for about 5 minutes.

Add the fish sauce, lime or lemon juice and salt and pepper to taste, then add the prawns and cook for a further 2–3 minutes until the prawns have turned pink.

Serve into bowls and top each bowl with some melted butter and chopped coriander.

Good-quality, large prawns have plenty of flavour, but do buy raw prawns. You will know they are cooked when they turn pink. The spices in this dish add just the right amount of colour and flavour. It is another easy, yet impressive curry. Serve with either plain or dill rice (see page 128).

Burmese Prawn Curry

550 g/1¼ lb large raw prawns, peeled and deveined (see page 72)

2 tablespoons soy sauce

a dash of fish sauce

½ teaspoon turmeric powder

vegetable oil, for frying

1 large onion, peeled and chopped

4 garlic cloves, peeled and finely chopped

½ teaspoon chilli powder

1 fresh green chilli, deseeded and finely chopped

2.5 cm/1 inch piece of fresh ginger, peeled and grated

4 tomatoes, chopped

a handful of chopped fresh coriander leaves, plus whole leaves to garnish

salt

Serves 4–6

Put the prawns into a bowl with the soy sauce, fish sauce, turmeric and a little salt, mix well together and leave in the fridge for 30 minutes.

Heat a little vegetable oil in a frying pan and fry the onion, garlic and chilli powder for a couple of minutes.

Next, add the prawns, fresh chilli, ginger, tomatoes and chopped coriander and cook for 5 minutes.

Add a small amount of water and simmer, covered, for 10–15 minutes until the sauce is quite thick.

Serve garnished with coriander leaves.

Chickpeas are grown extensively in India, where they form an important part of the diet for vegetarians. Here they are added to rice and prawns for a meal in one.

Prawns with Rice and Chickpeas

20 large raw prawns, shell on

vegetable oil, for frying

1 onion, peeled and finely chopped

4 garlic cloves, peeled and crushed

1½ teaspoons cardamom powder

1 teaspoon cumin powder

5 fresh red chillies, deseeded and finely chopped

450 g/1 lb short-grain rice, washed and drained

4 tomatoes, skinned, deseeded and finely chopped

1 litre/1¾ pints chicken stock

300 g/11 oz cooked chickpeas

juice of 2 lemons

salt and freshly ground black pepper

fresh coriander leaves, to garnish

Remove the heads and shells of the prawns, leaving the tails on, and cut a slit down the back of each one. Take out and discard the black vein that runs through the prawn. Set the prawns aside.

Heat some vegetable oil in a large frying pan and fry the onion and garlic until browned, then add the cardamom, cumin and chillies and cook for a few minutes.

Stir in the rice until it is thoroughly mixed with the other ingredients, then stir in the tomatoes and add enough of the chicken stock to cover. Season, stir once and put on a lid. Cook on a low heat for about 20 minutes until all the liquid has been absorbed.

Stir in the chickpeas and set aside to keep warm.

In another pan, heat some oil and quickly stir-fry the prawns until they turn pink. Stir in the lemon juice, season with salt and pepper and mix the prawns into the rice and chickpeas.

Serve sprinkled with the coriander.

Serves 4–6

Fresh curry leaves really make this dish. If you cannot get hold of fresh leaves, you can use dried, which you can buy in most good Asian food shops.

Hot, Sweet Prawns

300 g/11 oz raw prawns, peeled and deveined (see page 72)

1½ teaspoons tamarind pulp

5 fresh green chillies, finely chopped

3 garlic cloves, peeled and finely chopped

1 teaspoon cumin seeds

vegetable oil, for frying

2 large onions, peeled and finely chopped

¾ teaspoon coriander powder

½ teaspoon cumin powder

½ teaspoon chilli powder

1 teaspoon garam masala powder

½ teaspoon turmeric powder

2 tomatoes, finely chopped

2 teaspoons soft brown sugar

10 fresh curry leaves

a handful of chopped fresh coriander leaves

salt

Serves 4–6

Soak the tamarind pulp in a small amount of water for 30 minutes.

Put the green chillies, garlic and cumin seeds into a food processor and whiz to form a paste.

Heat some vegetable oil in a frying pan and fry the onions until golden. Add the paste and cook for a couple of minutes.

Add the coriander, cumin, chilli, garam masala and turmeric powders and cook for 1 minute, then add the tomatoes and cook for another 5 minutes.

Stir in the sugar, the curry and coriander leaves and add salt to taste. Add some of the tamarind water to dilute the sauce a little, bring to the boil and cook for a few minutes.

Add the prawns and simmer for about 3 minutes or until the prawns are cooked.

These two ingredients go so well together. This is not a particularly hot dish, so may appeal to those a little wary of curries. If you cannot get fresh pineapple, tinned will do just as well, but drain it thoroughly.

Curried Prawns and Pineapple

400 g/14 oz cooked peeled prawns

1 fresh red chilli, finely chopped

1 fresh green chilli, finely chopped

10 shallots, peeled and finely chopped

10 blanched almonds, chopped

1 stalk of lemon grass, chopped

2.5 cm/1 inch piece of fresh ginger, peeled and grated

a little ghee or vegetable oil, for frying

a 400 ml/14 fl oz tin of coconut milk

1 small ripe pineapple, peeled, cored and cut into cubes

a dash of fish sauce

a handful of fresh coriander leaves

Serves 4–6

Put the chillies, shallots, almonds, lemon grass and ginger into a food processor and whiz to a paste.

Heat some ghee or vegetable oil in a frying pan or wok and fry the paste for a minute or so, then add the coconut milk and simmer for about 5 minutes.

Add the pineapple and simmer for another 5 minutes, then add the prawns to heat through. Add a little fish sauce to season and heat for a couple of minutes.

Just before serving, stir in the fresh coriander.

Colourful, healthy and quick, quick, quick!

You must use large, whole prawns for this dish to appreciate their flavour.

Stir-fried Prawns and Spinach

500 g/1 lb 2 oz large raw prawns, peeled and deveined (see page 72)

a dollop of ghee or clarified butter, for frying

3 garlic cloves, peeled and finely chopped

1 large onion, peeled and finely chopped

1 teaspoon garam masala powder

1 teaspoon coriander powder

1 teaspoon turmeric powder

a pinch of chilli powder, or to taste

a pinch of ground ginger, or to taste

1 tablespoon tomato purée

2 x 225 g/8 oz packs of fresh spinach leaves, washed and drained

Serves 4–6

Heat the ghee or clarified butter in a large frying pan, add the garlic and onion and fry gently until soft.

Add the spices and tomato purée and stir-fry for 4–5 minutes, then stir in the spinach leaves until they soften.

Add the prawns and stir-fry until they have turned pink and are coated with the softened spinach, spices and the sauce. Serve at once.

Prawn Kebabs

3 or 4 large, raw prawns, heads and shells removed, tails left on, per person

For the marinade

600 ml/1 pint tub of natural yoghurt

2 garlic cloves, peeled and crushed

2 teaspoons garam masala powder

2 heaped teaspoons coriander powder

salt and freshly ground black pepper

For the garnish

chopped fresh coriander leaves

1 crunchy spring onion, cut in half and finely sliced lengthways

1 or 2 fresh green chillies, finely chopped

½ lime per person, to serve

Serves 4–6

Mix together all the ingredients for the marinade. Devein the prawns (see page 72) and thread them onto skewers, then put in a dish, cover with the marinade and leave in the fridge for 2–3 hours.

Preheat the grill or barbecue, put the kebabs on a rack and cook for about 5 minutes, turning from time to time. If there is any marinade mixture left, use a pastry brush to baste the skewers with the mixture.

Once the kebabs are plated, sprinkle the garnish over them and serve with lime halves.

These take seconds to make. Great if visitors drop in at short notice.

These are a complete change from your normal fishcake. For a start, there is no potato bulking them out, so what you get are the flavours from all the individual ingredients. This makes them rather special.

Deep-fried Prawn Cakes

450 g/1 lb cooked peeled prawns

2 tablespoons Thai red curry paste

1 egg, beaten

1 tablespoon fish sauce

25 g/1 oz cornflour

vegetable oil, for deep-frying

Serves 4–6

Put the prawns, red curry paste, egg and fish sauce into a food processor and whiz until you have a smooth mixture.

Using your hands, make 12–20 cakes, depending on what size you prefer, and roll them in the cornflour.

Deep-fry the cakes in hot vegetable oil for 1½–2 minutes until they are a golden brown. Drain on kitchen paper and serve.

Thai Fishcakes with Sweet Chilli Sauce

500 g/1 lb 2 oz raw crab, lobster or prawns, chopped

200 g/7 oz skinned, boneless white fish, chopped

2 tablespoons Thai red or green curry paste

1 egg, beaten

1 tablespoon finely chopped fresh coriander

a couple of dashes of fish sauce

1 teaspoon baking powder

2 fresh green chillies, finely chopped

1 tablespoon brown sugar

3 or 4 garlic cloves, peeled and crushed

2 fresh or dried Kaffir lime leaves, very finely chopped

75 g/3 oz frozen petits pois

plain flour, for dusting

vegetable oil, for deep-frying

Serves 4–6

Coarsely purée the seafood and fish in a food processor, then mix the processed fish with all the other ingredients except the flour and vegetable oil.

Form the mixture into small, bite-sized cakes and dust them in the flour.

Heat the oil in a large pan and deep-fry the fishcakes until golden.

Serve with Sweet Chilli Sauce (see page 141) and Floyd's Salad (see page 125).

Squid is a wonderful thing! Just do not overcook it – it will turn rubbery if you do.

Squid in a Hot Sauce

1 kg/2¼ lb squid, cleaned and sliced into rings

1 tablespoon white wine vinegar

6 blanched almonds, chopped

6 fresh red chillies, finely chopped

1 cm/½ inch piece of fresh ginger, peeled and grated

1 cm/½ inch stalk of lemon grass, crushed

6 shallots, peeled and finely chopped

½ teaspoon cumin powder

½ teaspoon turmeric powder

vegetable oil, for frying

3 tablespoons tamarind water (see page 44)

1 teaspoon soft brown sugar

salt

fresh coriander leaves, to garnish

Serves 4–6

Add the vinegar to 750 ml/1¼ pints of water, then rinse the squid in the water, drain and set aside.

Put the almonds, chillies, ginger, lemon grass and shallots into a food processor and whiz until you have a smooth paste. Add the spices and mix well.

Heat some vegetable oil in a pan. Add the spicy paste and fry for 1 minute, stirring all the time, then add the squid and the tamarind water. Cook for a couple of minutes, then add the sugar and salt to taste.

Simmer for 5 minutes, stirring all the time.

Garnish with coriander leaves and serve hot.

As with other recipes, do not overcook the prawns and squid. They literally take only a couple of minutes.

Squid and Prawns in Turmeric Gravy

200 g/7 oz squid, cut into squares and scored over the surface

300 g/11 oz raw prawns, peeled and deveined (see page 72)

1 small courgette, cut into strips and blanched in boiling water for 1 minute

150 g/5 oz fine green beans, blanched in boiling water for 1 minute

1 large fresh red chilli, deseeded and cut into fine strips

1 large fresh green chilli, deseeded and cut into fine strips

a 400 ml/14 fl oz tin of coconut milk

salt and freshly ground black pepper

For the turmeric gravy

10 large fresh red chillies, deseeded and chopped

5 shallots, peeled and finely chopped

2.5 cm/1 inch piece of fresh ginger, peeled and grated

1 tablespoon turmeric powder

vegetable oil, for frying

50 ml/2 fl oz tamarind water (see page 44)

250 ml/8½ fl oz fish stock

Serves 4–6

To prepare the turmeric gravy, put the chillies, shallots, ginger and turmeric into a food processor and whiz until smooth.

Heat a little vegetable oil in a frying pan and add the paste. Stir-fry for about 4 minutes, then add the tamarind water and fish stock.

Bring to the boil and simmer for 10 minutes until the gravy thickens a little.

Add the squid and prawns, the vegetables and chillies and simmer for a couple of minutes, then add the coconut milk and stir over the heat for another couple of minutes to heat through. Season with salt and pepper to taste, then serve.

This dish is quite hot – there are a lot of chillies in there! You could use less if you wish, but if you have the stamina, be brave and follow the recipe. It will be really tangy.

82 | Bream in Ginger, Chilli and Tomato

4 good-sized bream fillets

1 teaspoon salt

a pinch of freshly ground black pepper

a good handful of fresh coriander leaves, chopped

vegetable oil, for frying

8 cherry tomatoes

4 fresh bird's eye chillies, left whole

8 sprigs of lemon basil

For the sauce

vegetable oil for frying

10 fresh red chillies, deseeded and finely chopped

8 garlic cloves, peeled and finely chopped

4 cm/1½ inch piece of fresh ginger, peeled and grated

2 stalks of lemon grass, crushed

2 Kaffir lime leaves, torn

salt

Serves 4–6

To prepare the sauce, heat some vegetable oil in a frying pan and add the chillies, garlic and ginger. Stir-fry over a low heat for about 3 minutes to release the flavours.

Add the lemon grass, lime leaves, salt to taste and 375 ml/13 fl oz of water and simmer for about 10 minutes.

Remove the lemon grass and lime leaves and whiz the sauce in a food processor until smooth. Set aside.

Season the bream fillets with the salt, pepper and coriander leaves.

In another pan, heat some oil and flash-fry the fish on both sides for 2 minutes a side.

Add the tomatoes and cook for 30 seconds, then add the prepared sauce and the whole bird's eye chillies. Simmer for a couple of minutes, then add the basil sprigs and serve.

In Thailand the dishes are simple, but quite hot. This dish takes minutes to make and the flavours perfectly complement the mussels without overpowering them.

Thai Mussels

700 g/1½ lb mussels in their shells, scrubbed, washed and debearded

vegetable oil, for frying

3 shallots, peeled and finely chopped

3 garlic cloves, peeled and finely chopped

1 tablespoon soy bean paste (available from Asian shops)

2.5 cm/1 inch piece of fresh ginger, peeled and grated

1 fresh red chilli, finely chopped

1 teaspoon brown sugar

Serves 4–6

Heat some vegetable oil in a large pan and gently fry the shallots and the garlic until slightly browned.

Stir in the soy bean paste until well combined, then add the ginger, chilli and mussels and stir-fry together for about 1 minute, then add the sugar.

Cover the pan and cook for about 5 minutes until all the mussels have opened. Discard any mussels that have not opened. Serve the mussels in individual bowls with the cooking liquid poured over them.

A very quick, simple, spicy dish that is ideal to pop onto the middle of the table and share with friends. However, as with all dishes containing mussels, do discard any that have not opened after cooking – or else!

Fragrant (Hot) Mussels

1.5–2 kg/3½–4½ lb mussels in their shells, scrubbed, washed and debearded

vegetable oil, for frying

1 large onion, peeled and finely chopped

1 small head of garlic, peeled and finely chopped

2.5 cm/1 inch piece of fresh ginger, peeled and finely grated

2 or 3 fresh green chillies, finely chopped

½ tablespoon cumin powder

1 teaspoon turmeric powder

a 400 ml/14 fl oz tin of coconut milk

chopped fresh coriander and parsley, to garnish

Serves 4–6

Heat some vegetable oil in a large pan and sauté the onion until soft. Then add the garlic, ginger, chillies and spices and cook for 2–3 minutes, stirring all the while.

Add the mussels, with no liquid, and stir into the pot, making sure they are all covered with the mixture.

Stir in the coconut milk, pop on the lid and cook gently until the mussels have opened. Stir two or three times to mix the natural liquor with the sauce. Discard any mussels that don't open.

Pour into a large bowl or individual bowls, sprinkle with the coriander and parsley and serve hot.

Mustard seeds make for a wonderful flavour, quite different from processed mustard, so do not be put off by them!

Fish in Spiced Gravy

700 g/1½ lb firm white fish fillets (such as cod, halibut or monkfish)

2 tablespoons poppy seeds

2 tablespoons mustard seeds

¼ fresh coconut, diced, or 50 g/2 oz desiccated coconut (if using dried, soak in water for 15 minutes and then squeeze dry)

1 cm/½ inch piece of fresh ginger, peeled and chopped

6 garlic cloves, peeled and finely chopped

1 teaspoon turmeric powder

1 onion, peeled and coarsely chopped

2 teaspoons coriander powder

1 teaspoon chilli powder

2–3 fresh green chillies

2 teaspoons cumin powder

vegetable oil, for frying

3 tomatoes, puréed or 1½ tablespoons tomato purée

juice of ½ lime

salt

a good handful of fresh coriander leaves or herbs of your choice, to garnish

Serves 4–6

Clean the fish fillets, salt them and leave to one side.

Toast the poppy seeds in a dry pan gently over a low heat for 2 minutes, then take off the heat, add a little water and leave for 15 minutes. Then pound to a paste in a pestle and mortar.

Put the poppy seeds, mustard seeds, coconut, ginger, garlic, turmeric, onion, coriander and chilli powders, green chillies, cumin and 1 teaspoon of salt into a food processor and whiz together. Add a little water to form a paste.

Fry the spice paste in a little vegetable oil for 5–6 minutes, stirring and adding water little by little as required, so it is not too dry.

Add the tomatoes and cook for 5 minutes, then pour in 300 ml/½ pint of water, the lime juice and salt to taste.

Add the fish and cook until done. Garnish with fresh herbs and serve.

Steaming fish does help to keep its texture and flavour, and it also preserves the flavour of the spices.

Steamed Fish Curry

450 g/1 lb firm white fish fillets (see page 85), thinly sliced

a good handful of spinach leaves

a few sprigs of fresh basil

a few sprigs of fresh mint

2 eggs, beaten

a 400 ml/14 fl oz tin of coconut milk

2 tablespoons fish sauce

3 tablespoons Thai red curry paste

1 fresh red chilli, deseeded and finely chopped

1 fresh green chilli, deseeded and finely chopped

a good handful of fresh coriander leaves, chopped

4 Kaffir lime leaves, torn

Serves 4–6

Using a dish that will fit in a steamer, line the dish with the spinach, basil and mint leaves.

Mix together the eggs, coconut milk, fish sauce and curry paste and stir well. Fold the fish slices into this and pour into the lined dish.

Sprinkle the chillies, coriander and lime leaves on top, cover and steam for 15–20 minutes.

Serve with rice of your choice (see pages 128–132).

This is an unusual dish – the fish is marinated and then fried before being cooked in a rich, red sauce in the oven.

Egyptian Fish Curry

900 g/2 lb firm white fish fillets (see page 85), cut into 4 cm/1½ inch squares

olive oil

juice of 1 lemon

2 pinches of saffron strands

vegetable oil, for frying

2 onions, peeled and coarsely chopped

3–4 garlic cloves, peeled and crushed

2 green peppers, deseeded and coarsely chopped

450 ml/¾ pint tomato passata (tomato sauce from a jar or can)

3 dried bird's eye chillies, crumbled

1 teaspoon cumin powder

seasoned flour

salt and freshly ground black pepper

Serves 4–6

Marinate the fish in enough olive oil to coat it lightly, the lemon juice and 1 pinch of the saffron strands for about 40 minutes.

Heat some vegetable oil in a frying pan and fry the onions, garlic and green peppers until they are nearly cooked, but still have texture.

Add the tomato passata, chillies, cumin and the remaining saffron, season with salt and pepper and cook until the sauce has reduced by about a fifth, has thickened and is rich red in colour.

Remove the fish from the marinade, dry on kitchen paper, dredge in the seasoned flour and fry on both sides in hot oil until golden on the outside.

Preheat the oven to 200°C/400°F/mark 6. Put half the tomato sauce in the bottom of a shallow ovenproof dish, layer the fish pieces on top and cover with the remaining sauce.

Bake in the oven for about 15 minutes, then serve.

This is a great way to serve firm fish. It has a definite taste of Asia about it and is a very quick dish to cook.

Bass is a very robust fish, with enough flavour to carry off this surprisingly simple but very flavoursome sauce.

Malaysian Fish Curry

450 g/1 lb firm white fish fillets (see page 85), cut into cubes

1 tablespoon anchovy essence

1 fresh red chilli, deseeded and very finely chopped

vegetable oil, for frying

1 onion, peeled and grated

4 Kaffir lime leaves

2 tablespoons Thai red curry paste

1 teaspoon fennel seeds

1 teaspoon cumin seeds

1 tablespoon coriander seeds, crushed

4 spring onions, finely sliced

1 garlic clove, peeled and finely chopped

juice of 1 lime

Serves 4–6

Put the fish, anchovy essence and chilli into a large bowl, mix together and leave in the fridge for about 30 minutes.

Heat a little vegetable oil in a frying pan and sauté the onion until soft.

Add the lime leaves, red curry paste and 300 ml/½ pint of water and bring to the boil, stirring all the time.

Add the fennel, cumin and coriander seeds and simmer for 5–8 minutes.

In another pan, fry the spring onions and garlic in a little oil and set aside.

Fry the fish in hot oil for a couple of minutes until just cooked. Drain and place in the sauce, then simmer gently for a couple of minutes. Add the lime juice and pour into a serving dish. Garnish with the garlic and spring onions and serve hot.

Chilli Bass with Garlic Sauce

1 whole sea bass (about 450 g/1 lb in weight), scaled and gutted

50 g/2 oz plain flour

vegetable oil, for frying

10 garlic cloves, peeled and finely chopped

4 fresh red chillies, deseeded and finely chopped

4 fresh green chillies, deseeded and finely chopped

2 spring onions, finely chopped

1 teaspoon coriander powder

3 tablespoons brown sugar

juice of 1 lime

juice of 1 lemon

90 ml/3 fl oz fish sauce

a good handful of fresh basil leaves, chopped

white pepper

Serves 4–6

Preheat the oven to 140°C/275°F/ mark 1. Clean the fish under running water and pat dry. Dip the fish in the flour on both sides.

Heat some vegetable oil in a large frying pan and shallow-fry the fish for about 5 minutes on each side, then remove the fish from the pan and put in the oven to keep warm.

Heat some more oil in another pan, throw in the garlic, chillies, spring onions and coriander powder and stir-fry for 2–3 minutes over a fairly low heat.

Stir in the sugar, lime and lemon juices, fish sauce and basil and simmer for about 2 minutes. Season the sauce with the pepper, pour over the fish and serve.

The sultanas in this recipe add a subtle sweetness to the lovely oven-baked fish.

Goan Bream with Onions and Sultanas

1 bream (about 1 kg/2¼ lb in weight), scaled, gutted and cleaned

vegetable oil, for frying

1 large onion, peeled and finely chopped

250 g/9 oz sultanas

1 fresh green chilli, very finely chopped

a pinch of freshly grated nutmeg

½ teaspoon ground ginger

1 teaspoon cinnamon powder

1 large bunch of parsley

salt

Serves 4–6

Make cuts in the fish on both sides and put to one side.

Heat some vegetable oil in a pan and fry the onion with a little salt.

Blanch the sultanas in boiling water for a few seconds and drain, then add to the onion and cook for another minute.

Preheat the oven to 180°C/350°F/mark 4. Mix the chilli, nutmeg, ginger and cinnamon with some oil and rub this mixture all over the fish. Put the parsley in the bottom of a shallow, ovenproof dish and put the fish on top. Cover the fish with the onion and sultanas and pour about 200 ml/7 fl oz of water into the dish.

Bake the fish in the oven for about 40 minutes until the sultanas and onion have turned golden and formed a crust and the fish is cooked.

This is quick and easy to make and is ideal for lunch or a swift snack.

The vegetables in this dish are steamed to keep their texture. It is a light, simple and healthy dish that should appeal to everyone.

Hot Fish Balls with Cucumber Relish

Hot and Sour Fish

750 g/1 lb 10 oz white fish fillets, skinned, washed and cubed

2 garlic cloves, peeled

a large handful of fresh coriander leaves

18–20 mixed peppercorns

3 dried red chillies, crumbled

½ teaspoon caster sugar

1 tablespoon plain flour

1 tablespoon soy sauce

vegetable oil, for deep-frying

For the cucumber relish

½ cucumber, peeled, deseeded and finely chopped

2 shallots, peeled and very finely chopped

1 small carrot, very finely chopped

1 teaspoon red wine vinegar

1 teaspoon sugar

Serves 4–6

]To make the relish, mix together all the ingredients and set aside in the fridge.

Put the garlic, coriander, peppercorns, chillies and sugar into a food processor and whiz to a paste.

Add the fish to the paste and whiz in the food processor until smooth, then add the flour and soy sauce and whiz again to combine.

Using your hands, shape the mixture into golf-ball-sized balls.

Heat about 4 cm/1½ inches of vegetable oil in a frying pan and deep-fry the fish balls until they are golden. Remove from the pan and drain on kitchen paper.

Serve hot with the cucumber relish.

450 g/1 lb firm, white fish fillets (see page 85)

vegetable oil, for deep-frying

2 garlic cloves, peeled and finely chopped

225 g/8 oz okra, chopped into 1 cm/ ½ inch pieces

225 g/8 oz tomatoes, cut into quarters

2 fresh red chillies, deseeded and finely chopped

1 small tin of pineapple chunks in juice

a few slices of white radish

1 onion, peeled, finely sliced and fried until crisp

5 or 6 fresh curry leaves

a good handful of fresh basil leaves

Serves 4–6

Heat about 2.5 cm/1 inch of vegetable oil in a deep pan and fry the fish fillets and garlic in batches for 3–4 minutes. Do not overcrowd the pan. Drain and keep in a warm place.

Steam the okra, tomatoes, chillies, pineapple and radish for about 5 minutes to keep their texture and put on a serving dish.

Lay the fish fillets over the vegetables and sprinkle on the fried onions, curry leaves and basil leaves.

If you can't find banana leaves (Asian stores sell them), use large
pieces of kitchen foil instead. The aim is to seal in all the flavour.

Curried Fish in Banana Leaf

1 fresh whole fish
(about 1 kg/2¼ lb in
weight), such as
salmon or trout,
scaled, gutted
and washed

2 teaspoons crushed
coriander seeds

2 teaspoons
cumin seeds

1 tablespoon grated,
fresh coconut (if using
dried, see page 85)

½ teaspoon
turmeric powder

2 fresh red chillies,
deseeded and
finely chopped

1 onion, peeled
and grated

2 garlic cloves, peeled
and crushed

a handful of
chopped fresh
coriander leaves

1 tablespoon tamarind
water (see page 44) or
lemon juice

1 tablespoon
vegetable oil

2 or 3 banana leaves

salt

Serves 4–6

Grind the coriander and cumin seeds with a little salt in a pestle and
mortar, then pound up with the coconut.

Add the turmeric, chillies, onion, garlic and coriander leaves and mix
well, then add the tamarind water or lemon juice and the vegetable oil
and mix to make a paste.

Make several incisions along the top of the fish and rub in the paste,
then rub it inside the cavity of the fish. Marinate in the fridge for about
3 hours.

Preheat the oven to 220°C/425°F/mark 7. Grease the banana leaves
and wrap them around the fish. (You can use foil wrapped loosely
around the fish if you prefer.)

Bake in the oven for about 30 minutes, then unwrap the leaves or foil
and allow the fish to brown for a further 7–10 minutes.

All the different flavours in this curry are superb. I'm using Dijon mustard instead of mustard seeds – it's more subtle.

Fish Curry with Mustard

550 g/1¼ lb firm white fish fillets (see page 85)

2 tablespoons poppy seeds

1 tablespoon Dijon mustard

1 teaspoon turmeric powder

2 tablespoons grated fresh coconut (if using dried, see page 85)

5–6 garlic cloves, peeled

1 cm/½ inch piece of fresh ginger, peeled and grated

3 fresh green chillies

1 onion, peeled and chopped

2 teaspoons coriander powder

2 teaspoons cumin powder

1 teaspoon chilli powder

vegetable oil, for frying

250 ml/8½ fl oz fresh tomato purée

juice of ½ lime

salt

a handful of chopped fresh coriander leaves, to garnish

Serves 4–6

Toast the poppy seeds in a dry frying pan gently over a low heat for 2 minutes, then take off the heat and soak in water for 10–15 minutes. Pound to a paste in a pestle and mortar.

Put the poppy seeds, mustard, turmeric, coconut, garlic, ginger, fresh green chillies, onion, coriander, cumin and chilli powders and a little salt into a food processor and whiz to a paste, adding a little water to help the mixture along.

Heat a little vegetable oil in a large pan and fry the paste for 5 minutes, stirring and adding a little more water to make a sauce.

Add the tomato purée and stir-fry for another 5 minutes, then add more water and the lime juice and simmer until you have a rich sauce.

Add the fish fillets and poach them in the sauce until they are cooked. Season, garnish with the coriander leaves and serve with plain rice.

Vegetable Curries

This may appear old-fashioned, but home-made mulligatawny soup is
the ideal antidote to a cold winter's day.

Mulligatawny Soup

60 g/2½ oz yellow
lentils, rinsed
and drained

60 g/2½ oz red
lentils, rinsed
and drained

1 red apple, peeled,
cored and quartered

1 cm/½ inch piece of
fresh ginger, peeled

1 cinnamon stick

1 fresh red
chilli, chopped

1 teaspoon
coriander seeds

¼ teaspoon
fenugreek seeds

½ teaspoon
cumin seeds

20 black peppercorns

3 cloves

6 curry leaves

juice of ½ lemon

salt and freshly
ground black pepper

a good handful of
chopped fresh
coriander leaves,
to garnish

Serves 4–6

Put all the ingredients except the lemon juice, salt and black pepper in
a large pan, cover with water and bring to the boil. Cover the pan and
simmer until the lentils are tender.

Remove from the heat, cool slightly and push through a sieve. Discard
any remnants left in the sieve. You should have a thickish mixture. Add
enough water to bring to the consistency of a soup.

Bring back to the boil, add the lemon juice and season with salt and
pepper, then serve garnished with the chopped coriander.

Don't be put off by the number of ingredients – this soup is quick and easy to make and it's not only green, it's very tasty. Dried shrimps and shrimp paste are usually both available in Asian supermarkets.

Green Vegetable Soup

500 g/1 lb 2 oz mixed green leaves (such as spring cabbage, spinach, pak choi or any Asian leaves, mustard greens, watercress, etc.), coarsely chopped

1.4 litres/2½ pints weak chicken stock

1 onion, peeled and very finely chopped

2 or 3 garlic cloves, peeled and finely chopped

100 g/3½ oz dried shrimps

1 teaspoon shrimp paste

2 or 3 fresh green chillies, very finely chopped

1 stalk of fresh lemon grass, chopped, or dried lemon grass

a dash of soy sauce

a dash of fish sauce

fresh coriander and mint leaves, to garnish

Serves 4–6

Bring the chicken stock to the boil, then add the onion, garlic, dried shrimps, shrimp paste, green chillies and lemon grass and cook for 5 minutes or so.

Add the chopped green leaves and soy and fish sauces to taste and cook for 4–5 minutes.

Serve hot, garnished with fresh coriander and mint leaves.

This rich, warming, tangy soup makes a delicious starter or a substantial main meal. If you are vegetarian, you can substitute vegetable stock for the chicken stock.

Lentil and Mint Soup

200 g/7 oz red or yellow lentils, rinsed and drained

unsalted butter and olive oil, for frying

1 large red onion, peeled and finely chopped

2 or 3 garlic cloves, peeled and finely chopped

2 tomatoes, deseeded and finely chopped

2 fresh red chillies, finely chopped

1 heaped tablespoon tomato purée

2 tablespoons paprika

25 g/1 oz long-grain rice

1 tablespoon dried mint

1 litre/1¾ pints chicken stock

salt and freshly ground black pepper

For the garnish

2 fresh red chillies, very, very finely chopped

shredded fresh mint leaves

100 g/3½ oz unsalted butter, melted

Serves 4–6

Heat a little butter and olive oil in a large pan. Stir in the onion and garlic and sauté gently until soft, then stir in the tomatoes and chillies and cook for a couple of minutes.

Add the tomato purée and the paprika, stir and cook for a couple of minutes, then add the lentils, rice, dried mint and chicken stock. Simmer gently for 30–40 minutes until you have a lovely soup. Taste and season with salt and pepper, and maybe add a little more dried mint. Pour into bowls.

For the garnish, stir the chillies and mint into the melted butter and swirl over each bowl of soup. Serve hot.

There are wonderful flavours and textures to this curry and it is surprisingly rich.

Mixed Dried Fruit Curry

100 g/3½ oz dried apricots

100 g/3½ oz blanched almonds

75 g/3 oz shelled pistachios

100 g/3½ oz cashew nuts

300 ml/½ pint tub of natural yoghurt

vegetable oil, for frying

1 cinnamon stick

3 cloves

3 onions, peeled and finely chopped

1 cm/½ inch piece of fresh ginger, peeled and chopped

4 garlic cloves, peeled and finely chopped

4 fresh green chillies, finely chopped

1 teaspoon coriander powder

½ teaspoon cumin powder

1 teaspoon chilli powder

2 tomatoes, chopped

75 g/3 oz walnut pieces

100 g/3½ oz seedless raisins

¼ teaspoon garam masala powder

salt

a pinch of white pepper

4 tablespoons single cream, to serve

Serves 4–6

Soak the apricots in water for 1½ hours until soft, then drain and reserve the water. Soak the almonds and pistachios in hot water for 1 hour. Drain, remove any skins and reserve the soaking water.

Grind half the cashew nuts, adding a little of the reserved water to make a paste.

Add salt and pepper to the yoghurt.

Heat some vegetable oil in a frying pan, add the cinnamon and cloves and fry briefly, then add the onions and fry until golden. Add the ginger, garlic and fresh chillies and cook for a few minutes.

Add the coriander powder and cook for a couple of minutes, then add the cumin and chilli powders and the tomatoes and cook for a couple of minutes.

Take off the heat, remove the cinnamon stick and whiz the mixture in a food processor to a purée. Pour into a pan, add the yoghurt, cashew paste and a little of the reserved water, season to taste and simmer with a lid on for 15 minutes.

In another frying pan, fry all the nuts in a little oil, including the remaining cashews, the raisins and apricots for 5–6 minutes. Add to the sauce and cook for another 10 minutes or so. Add the garam masala powder and cook for a few more minutes, then top with the cream and serve.

This is a wonderful, palate-cleansing, summer dish with bite. It makes a great starter, light but tangy.

Watermelon Curry

½ large watermelon, skinned, deseeded, and cut into 4 cm/ 1½ inch cubes

2 teaspoons chilli powder

1 teaspoon turmeric powder

1 teaspoon coriander powder

2 garlic cloves, peeled and puréed

vegetable oil, for frying

½ teaspoon cumin seeds

2 teaspoons sugar

juice of ½ lime

salt

1 fresh green chilli, deseeded and very finely chopped, to garnish

Serves 4–6

Take a handful of the chopped watermelon and whiz in a food processor to make a juice. Add this juice to the chilli, turmeric and coriander powders and the garlic purée and add salt to taste.

Heat a little vegetable oil in a pan, add the cumin seeds and cook for a few seconds, then add the spiced juice.

Reduce the heat and simmer for a few minutes until the liquid is reduced by a third.

Add the sugar and lime juice and cook for another minute, then add the watermelon cubes and cook on a very low heat for 4 minutes, stirring gently to coat the watermelon in the spices.

Serve sprinkled with the chopped chilli.

Asian dishes are very forgiving when it comes to ingredients. This combination of fruit and vegetables (you can use most of your favourite vegetables) is delicious and quick.

Mango and Vegetable Curry

approx. 100 g/3½ oz each of the following (or any other vegetable you like), all cut into bite-sized pieces: green beans, pumpkin, potato, onion, green bananas

1 large unripe mango, cut into bite-sized pieces

2½ dessertspoons turmeric powder

salt

fresh herbs, to garnish

For the masala (curry paste)

225 g/8 oz grated fresh coconut (if using dried, see page 85)

8 small shallots, peeled and chopped

5 fresh green chillies

1 teaspoon cumin seeds

6 fresh curry leaves

Serves 4–6

Put all the ingredients for the masala into a food processor and whiz until you have a paste (add a little water if the mixture is too dry).

Put the vegetable, banana and mango pieces into a large pan and add enough boiling water to cover. Stir in the turmeric and salt to taste and boil for 5–7 minutes.

When the vegetables are cooked, strain off the cooking liquid and put to one side.

Stir the masala spices into the cooked vegetables and add a small amount of the reserved cooking liquid, then continue to cook until you have a thick spicy gravy.

Serve sprinkled with a handful of fresh herbs.

Omelette Curry

3 eggs

1 onion, peeled and very finely chopped

2 fresh green chillies, very finely chopped

1 teaspoon chopped fresh coriander leaves

vegetable oil, for frying

salt and freshly ground black pepper

For the sauce

2 tablespoons grated fresh coconut (if using dried, see page 85)

½ teaspoon cumin seeds

½ teaspoon fennel seeds

2 teaspoons coriander powder

½ teaspoon chilli powder

½ teaspoon turmeric powder

½ teaspoon garam masala powder

3 onions, peeled and finely chopped

3 fresh green chillies, finely chopped

2 tomatoes, finely chopped

1 teaspoon red wine vinegar

a handful of chopped fresh coriander leaves

salt

Serves 4–6

To prepare the sauce, put the coconut, cumin and fennel seeds, coriander, chilli, turmeric and garam masala powders into a food processor and whiz together with a little water to make a paste. Set aside.

To make the omelette, whisk the eggs, add the onion, green chillies and coriander leaves and season to taste. Heat a little oil in a frying pan and pour in the omelette mixture. When the underneath is cooked, flip the omelette over and cook the other side until it is golden and well set. Remove from the heat and cut into strips, then roll up the strips and set aside.

To finish the sauce, heat some oil in a frying pan and fry the onions until they are soft and starting to brown. Add the spice paste and stir-fry for about 5 minutes.

Add the green chillies and tomatoes and sauté for 5 minutes, then add the vinegar, about 500 ml/18 fl oz of water and season to taste. Simmer for 10 minutes, then add the omelette strips and chopped coriander. Heat through for 3–4 minutes, then serve.

Paneer is an Indian form of cottage cheese but quite unlike cottage cheese as we know it. It is firm in texture, looking a little like tofu. It absorbs flavours well. Do try to get (or make) the real thing for this recipe. Nothing else will really do.

Paneer and Vegetable Curry

ghee or clarified butter, for frying

450 g/1 lb paneer (Indian cheese), cut into approx. 2.5 cm/ 1 inch cubes

1 red onion, peeled and finely sliced

1 teaspoon cumin powder

1 teaspoon ground ginger

½ teaspoon chilli powder

450 g/1 lb frozen peas

2 or 3 tomatoes, finely chopped

salt

Serves 4–6

Melt some ghee or clarified butter in a frying pan, add the paneer and fry until golden brown. Take out of the pan and set aside on kitchen paper to drain.

Add the onion to the pan and fry until soft and slightly coloured.

Add the spices and salt and fry for a couple more minutes to release the flavours, then add the peas and tomatoes and stir well until the vegetables are coated with the spicy mixture.

Add the paneer and stir well until all the ingredients are combined and the paneer is heated through. Serve.

Paneer goes well with spinach in this simple curry. Serve as a side dish or with some bread as a course in its own right.

Paneer with Spinach

400 g/14 oz paneer (Indian cheese; see page 107), cut into cubes

800 g/1¾ lb spinach, washed and well drained

ghee or clarified butter, for frying

1 teaspoon cumin seeds

3 garlic cloves, peeled and finely chopped

2 teaspoons coriander powder

1 teaspoon chilli powder

salt

100 ml/3½ fl oz double cream, to serve

Serves 4–6

Heat a little ghee or clarified butter in a frying pan and fry the cheese until golden brown on all sides. Set aside.

Stir-fry the spinach in a little ghee until well softened, then whiz to a purée in a food processor.

Heat some more ghee and add the cumin seeds and garlic and sauté until golden brown.

Add the coriander and chilli powders and the spinach, season and stir-fry for a couple of minutes, then add the paneer and simmer gently for about 5 minutes.

Put the mixture into a dish, top with the cream and serve.

Do take the trouble to find the right mushrooms for this dish. Button mushrooms do not have the necessary flavour. It may look like a complicated recipe, but it is really worth the trouble for that authentic Chinese taste.

Chilli Mushrooms with Cashew Nuts

350 g/12 oz oyster or Chinese mushrooms, chopped into bite-sized pieces

2.5 cm/1 inch piece of fresh ginger, peeled and grated

vegetable oil, for frying

4 garlic cloves, peeled and finely sliced

1 cm/½ inch piece of fresh ginger, peeled and finely sliced

2 dried chillies, crumbled

2 spring onions, cut into 2.5 cm/ 1 inch lengths

2 teaspoons cornflour

For the garnish

1 teaspoon sesame seeds

2 tablespoons cashew nuts, fried gently for about 1 minute

For the sauce

125 ml/4 fl oz chicken or strong vegetable stock

2 tablespoons chilli sauce

1 tablespoon Chinese black vinegar or balsamic vinegar

1 tablespoon dark soy sauce

2 teaspoons oyster sauce

1 teaspoon sesame oil

½ teaspoon Chinese five-spice powder

1 teaspoon sugar

Serves 4–6

Put the grated ginger in a small saucepan, cover with water and boil for about 1 minute. Strain and keep the water, discarding the ginger.

Blanch the mushrooms in the ginger water for about 1 minute, then drain well. Fry the mushrooms in hot vegetable oil for about 1 minute to seal, then drain and set aside.

Put all the sauce ingredients into a small bowl, mix together and set aside.

Heat some more oil in a wok or heavy-bottomed saucepan and stir-fry the garlic, sliced ginger and chillies for about 30 seconds.

Add the mushrooms and spring onions and stir-fry for about 1 minute, then add the sauce to the pan and cook for 1 minute.

Add the cornflour and cook for about 30 seconds to thicken the mixture.

Put on a serving dish and garnish with the sesame seeds and cashew nuts.

Almost everyone has eggs in their fridge and this is a great way of using them for the curry lover.

The tanginess and texture of green tomatoes is essential for this dish, and for those of you who grow your own tomatoes, this is a great way of using those that refuse to ripen. It can be eaten like a chutney, as an accompaniment, but also stands on its own as a main dish.

Curried Eggs

4 hard-boiled eggs, shelled and cut in half

chopped fresh coriander leaves, to garnish

For the masala (curry paste)

2 or 3 garlic cloves, peeled and crushed

2.5 cm/1 inch piece of fresh ginger, finely grated

1 teaspoon each of turmeric, cumin, fennel and chilli powders

1 tablespoon coriander powder

For the sauce

vegetable oil, for frying

1 teaspoon fenugreek seeds

1 teaspoon fennel seeds

1 small cinnamon stick

1 large onion, peeled and finely chopped

2 or 3 tomatoes, finely chopped

a 400 ml/14 fl oz tin of coconut milk

salt and freshly ground black pepper

Put all the ingredients for the masala with a little water into a food processor and whiz to a paste, then put to one side.

For the sauce, heat a little vegetable oil in a pan. Add the fenugreek and fennel seeds and the cinnamon stick and stir-fry for a couple of seconds. Add the onion and cook until soft, then stir in the tomatoes. Add the curry paste and stir-fry for a minute, then stir in the coconut milk and simmer until you have a smooth, rich gravy. If this appears to be too thick, thin with a little water. Season to taste.

Put the hard-boiled eggs gently into the gravy and heat to warm through. Serve garnished with the chopped coriander.

Serves 4–6

Curried Green Tomatoes

500 g/1 lb 2 oz unripe green tomatoes, chopped

1 teaspoon chilli powder

2 teaspoons coriander powder

1 teaspoon turmeric powder

2 garlic cloves, peeled and puréed

1 teaspoon sugar

vegetable oil, for frying

½ teaspoon cumin seeds

½ teaspoon fenugreek seeds

3 fresh green chillies, finely chopped

salt

Put the chilli, coriander and turmeric powders, the garlic and sugar into a small bowl, mix together and add a little water to form a paste.

Heat some vegetable oil in a large pan and fry the cumin and fenugreek seeds for a few seconds, then add the paste and cook for a couple of minutes.

Add the tomatoes and fresh chillies, season with salt and cook, stirring occasionally, until the tomatoes are softened.

Serves 4–6

This is a little bit of a variation on stuffed peppers. Do not overcook this dish as the tomatoes will collapse and lose some of their flavour. You can leave out the peanuts if you wish.

Hot Stuffed Tomatoes

4 large ripe tomatoes

a 400 g/14 oz tin of cooked lentils, rinsed and drained

150 g/5 oz paneer (Indian cheese, see page 107), grated

vegetable oil, for frying

1 tablespoon cumin seeds

1 cm/½ inch piece of fresh ginger, peeled and grated

1 teaspoon chilli powder

1 fresh green chilli, very finely chopped

1 dessertspoon chopped unsalted peanuts

1 teaspoon sugar

a handful of chopped fresh coriander leaves, plus extra to garnish

salt

Serves 4–6

Preheat the oven to 200°C/400°F/mark 6. Put the lentils into a food processor and whiz enough to break them down. Then put them into a bowl and mix with the paneer.

Cut the tops off the tomatoes and scoop out and reserve the flesh.

Heat a little vegetable oil in a heavy-bottomed pan and add the cumin seeds, ginger, chilli powder, fresh chilli, peanuts, sugar, chopped coriander and salt. Fry for about 1 minute, then add the tomato flesh and cook for another minute.

Add the lentils and paneer and mix well together for another couple of minutes.

Stuff the tomatoes with the lentil mixture and cook in the oven for about 10 minutes.

Serve hot, garnished with the chopped coriander leaves.

Although the sauce is a little fiddly, this is a delicious vegetable dish and worth the trouble.

Vegetable Brochettes with Tofu and Cinnamon

1 courgette, cut into slices of medium thickness

1 large onion, peeled and cut into wedges

1 red pepper, cut into 2.5 cm/1 inch squares

vegetable oil, for frying

1–2 cakes firm tofu, cut into 2.5 cm/ 1 inch square chunks

8–10 button mushrooms

For the sauce

2 garlic cloves, peeled and finely chopped

4 shallots, peeled and finely chopped

2.5 cm/1 inch piece of fresh ginger, peeled and grated

1 fresh red chilli, finely chopped

1 fresh green chilli, finely chopped

125 ml/4 fl oz chicken stock

2 tablespoons Thai sweet soy sauce

2 tablespoons coriander seeds, toasted and crushed

½ teaspoon coriander powder

½ teaspoon cinnamon powder

½ teaspoon freshly grated nutmeg

½ teaspoon white pepper

a pinch of ground cloves

salt

Serves 4–6

Blanch the courgette slices, onion wedges and pepper squares in boiling water for 2 minutes, remove and drain.

Heat a little vegetable oil in a pan and fry the tofu on all sides until it is golden brown.

To make the sauce, heat some oil in a small pan and stir-fry the garlic, shallots, ginger and chillies until they have softened.

Add all the other sauce ingredients and bring to the boil, then reduce the heat and simmer until the sauce reduces by about half. Cool, then whiz in a food processor until smooth.

Thread alternate pieces of courgette, red pepper, onion, mushroom and tofu onto skewers and brush with the sauce.

Cook on a barbecue, under a hot grill or on a griddle, turning the skewers until the vegetables have cooked.

This is a wonderfully colourful, spicy and filling dish, whether you are
vegetarian or not!

Red or Green Peppers Stuffed with Spicy Lentils

4 red or green peppers with their tops cut off (retain the tops), deseeded and pith removed

a 400 g/14 oz tin of cooked lentils, rinsed and drained

ghee, butter or vegetable oil, for frying

2 red onions, peeled and finely diced

2 or 3 fresh green chillies, finely chopped

2.5 cm/1 inch piece of fresh ginger, peeled and finely grated

1 teaspoon cumin seeds

3 teaspoons freshly ground coriander seeds

salt and freshly ground black pepper

chopped fresh coriander leaves, to garnish

Serves 4–6

Heat some ghee, butter or vegetable oil in a pan and gently fry the onions, chillies and ginger until they are soft.

Stir in the spices, season with salt and pepper and cook for about 5 minutes, until all the ingredients are well amalgamated, then remove from the heat and mix in the lentils.

Preheat the oven to 190°C/375°F/mark 5. Stuff the peppers with the lentil and spice mixture, replace the lids of the peppers and paint them generously with ghee, butter or oil. Put the peppers in a baking dish and cover lightly with tin foil. Bake in the oven for about 30 minutes, basting from time to time with more butter or ghee.

Serve garnished with chopped coriander.

These barely need an introduction – we all order them when we are at the local Indian restaurant. But they are so simple to make, and they are so much more delicious than anything you can buy.

A lovely, creamy dish that can be eaten either as a starter or as a vegetable accompaniment to a main dish.

Onion Bhajis

2 onions, peeled and finely sliced

100 g/3½ oz chickpea flour, sifted to remove any lumps

1 teaspoon coriander powder

1 teaspoon cumin powder

2 fresh green chillies, deseeded and finely chopped

vegetable oil, for deep-frying

salt

Serves 4–6

Put the flour, coriander and cumin powders, the chillies, a little vegetable oil and warm water and salt to taste into a food processor and whiz until you have a smooth batter.

Put the batter aside for about 30 minutes, then stir in the onion slices.

Heat the vegetable oil in a deep-fat fryer, then gently drop spoonfuls of the batter mixture into the pan – about 3 at a time. When they are golden, lift out and drain on kitchen paper. Serve hot as a starter or as a main course with salad.

Spiced Baby Onions in Yoghurt

500 g/1 lb 2 oz baby onions, peeled and cut into quarters

1 teaspoon chilli powder

2 teaspoons coriander powder

2 teaspoons turmeric powder

50 ml/2 fl oz natural yoghurt

vegetable oil, for frying

1 teaspoon cumin seeds

2 garlic cloves, peeled and crushed

2.5 cm/1 inch piece of fresh ginger, peeled and grated

salt

Serves 4–6

Mix together the chilli, coriander and turmeric powders and the yoghurt with a little water and put to one side.

Heat some oil in a pan and cook the cumin seeds for a few seconds, then stir in the garlic and ginger and stir-fry for a few seconds.

Add the yoghurt mixture and the onions, stirring to coat them well.

Add about 1½ cups of water and simmer over a low heat until the onions are tender. Add salt to taste.

Even the most common, simple vegetables make wonderful curries. They are healthy since they are generally cooked very quickly, thus retaining the nutrients. As with all curries, you can make them hotter or milder as you prefer.

Okra, or ladies' fingers, are a delicious vegetable, now widely available. They are wonderful in curries, but be aware when you cook them that they initially appear to go rather sticky – don't panic! As they cook, the stickiness goes.

Carrots and Cauliflower with Chilli and Ginger

Spiced Okra

6 or 7 carrots,
sliced into rounds, or
baby carrots left whole

200 g/7 oz
cauliflower florets

vegetable oil, for
frying

3 shallots, peeled and
finely sliced

1 or 2 garlic cloves,
peeled and
finely sliced

4 spring onions,
sliced into 2.5 cm/
1 inch lengths

1 tablespoon light
soy sauce

a dash of fish sauce

1 fresh red chilli,
finely chopped

a pinch of
ground ginger

Serves 4–6

Blanch the carrots and cauliflower in boiling water for about 3 minutes, then drain and set aside.

Heat some vegetable oil in a wok or frying pan and fry the shallots for a minute or two until soft, then add the garlic and fry for a further minute, taking care not to burn the garlic.

Add the spring onions, soy and fish sauces, carrots and cauliflower and stir-fry for a couple of minutes.

Finally, add the chilli and ginger and stir-fry for 2 minutes more. Serve hot.

400 g/14 oz okra,
washed and cut
into chunks

vegetable oil, for
frying

½ teaspoon garam
masala powder

2.5 cm/1 inch piece
of fresh ginger, peeled
and grated

1 teaspoon
turmeric powder

1 fresh green chilli,
finely chopped

300 ml/½ pint natural
yoghurt

a good handful of
fresh coriander,
roughly chopped

salt

Serves 4–6

Heat a little vegetable oil in a saucepan, add the garam masala powder and stir-fry for a few seconds until the aroma is released, then add the okra. Fry for about 5 minutes, stirring, then add the ginger, turmeric, chilli and salt to taste. Stir-fry for about another minute.

Add a little water to moisten, then cook gently, stirring occasionally, until the okra is cooked.

Stir in the yoghurt and heat through.

At the last minute, stir in the coriander and serve hot.

Home-made dal makes a wonderful side dish to most curries. Eaten with naan bread or roti (see pages 133, 135), it makes a spicy, creamy starter dish.

Spicy Dal

200 g/7 oz green lentils, rinsed and drained	Put the lentils in a pan, cover with water and add the turmeric and salt to taste. Cook until tender.
1 teaspoon turmeric powder	
vegetable oil, for frying	Heat a little vegetable oil in a pan and add the cumin seeds. Fry for a couple of minutes, then add the onions and stir-fry until brown. Stir in the ginger, garlic and chilli powder, then add the tomatoes.
1 teaspoon cumin seeds	
2 red onions, peeled and finely chopped	
2.5 cm/1 inch piece of fresh ginger, peeled and grated	Cook this sauce for about 20 minutes until puréed, then add the lentils and simmer for 5–7 minutes.
2 garlic cloves, peeled and crushed	
1 dessertspoon chilli powder	
3 tomatoes, finely chopped	
salt	

Serves 4–6

Cauliflower is not the most flavoursome vegetable around, but soaks up other flavours very well. This makes either a substantial side dish or a main course.

Cauliflower Dal

500 g/1 lb 2 oz cauliflower florets	Heat a little vegetable oil in a saucepan and gently fry the onions, garlic, ginger, chillies and spices until the onions have softened.
vegetable oil, for frying	
2 red onions, peeled and finely chopped	Add the lentils and stock and simmer for about 10 minutes.
2 garlic cloves, peeled and finely chopped	
2.5 cm/1 inch piece of fresh ginger, peeled and grated	Add the cauliflower and coconut milk to the lentils, then simmer for another 10 minutes.
4 fresh red chillies, finely chopped	
1 teaspoon coriander powder	Stir in the peas, chopped coriander and lemon juice, bring to a simmer and cook for a couple of minutes or until the peas are cooked. Season with salt and serve.
1 teaspoon cumin powder	
½ teaspoon garam masala powder	
75 g/3 oz small green lentils, rinsed and drained	
300 ml/½ pint vegetable stock	
a 400 ml/14 fl oz tin of coconut milk	
130 g/4½ oz peas	
a good handful of fresh coriander leaves, chopped	
juice of ½ lemon	
salt	

Serves 4–6

For this recipe from Singapore you must use firm tofu. It has little flavour itself, but soaks up other flavours like a sponge. The rich peanut sauce is perfect in this dish.

Chillied Tofu Salad with Peanut Sauce

400 g/14 oz firm tofu, drained and cut into 2.5 cm/1 inch cubes

vegetable oil, for frying

1 dried red chilli

50 g/2 oz cucumber, deseeded and cut into 4 cm/1½ inch strips

50 g/2 oz carrot, peeled and cut into 4 cm/1½ inch strips

50 g/2 oz fine green beans, topped, tailed and blanched for 1 minute

2 spring onions, cut into 4 cm/ 1½ inch strips

mixed salad leaves

1 fresh red chilli, deseeded and cut into very fine strips

1 tablespoon coarsely chopped peanuts, to garnish

For the peanut sauce

100 g/3½ oz unsalted peanuts

4 garlic cloves, peeled

1 large fresh red chilli

1½ tablespoons soft brown sugar

4 teaspoons white wine vinegar

3 tablespoons dark soy sauce

Serves 4–6

Put all the ingredients for the peanut sauce with 125 ml/4 fl oz of water into a food processor and whiz until you have a thick, smooth sauce. Set aside.

Heat some vegetable oil in a heavy-bottomed saucepan, add the dried red chilli and stir to release its flavour into the oil.

Add the tofu cubes to the oil and fry for about 4 minutes, turning them regularly, until they are golden brown. Drain on kitchen paper and discard the dried chilli.

Mix the tofu with all the salad ingredients and the fresh chilli and add to the bowl of peanut sauce. Toss the mixture together, then transfer to a serving dish, sprinkle over the chopped peanuts and serve.

Particularly in Malaysia, salads are very popular and they can be warm, as this one is, or cold. The addition of nuts makes for a crunchy texture, but you can leave them out if you prefer.

Hot Salad with Peanut Sauce

1 potato, peeled and finely sliced

vegetable oil for frying

100 g/3½ oz each of:
shredded cabbage;
cauliflower florets;
runner beans, sliced;
baby carrots, sliced;
bean sprouts

For the peanut sauce

vegetable oil for frying

100 g/ 3½ oz
unsalted peanuts

1 garlic clove, peeled
and very finely
chopped

2 shallots, peeled and
very finely chopped

a dash of fish sauce

1 small fresh green
chilli, very finely
chopped

1 teaspoon
brown sugar

a 250 ml/8½ fl oz
carton of coconut
cream

lemon juice

salt

For the garnish

½ cucumber, peeled
and finely sliced

2 tablespoons
chopped peanuts

1 onion, peeled, finely
sliced and fried
until crispy

Serves 4–6

To make the sauce, heat some vegetable oil in a frying pan or wok and fry the peanuts for 5 minutes, stirring all the time. Drain the peanuts on kitchen paper, then whiz to a powder in a food processor.

Using a pestle and mortar, pound the garlic, shallots, fish sauce and chilli to a fine paste, using a little salt to help the process. Fry this paste in a little oil for 1 minute, stirring all the time, then add the sugar and 400 ml/14 fl oz of water and bring to the boil.

Add the peanut powder and simmer until the mixture has thickened, then add the coconut cream, stirring well until all the ingredients are well mixed. Set aside, keeping the sauce warm.

To make the salad, fry the potato slices in a little vegetable oil until crisp and brown. Blanch the other vegetables in boiling water for 4–5 minutes, then drain and set aside.

Arrange the cucumber slices on one side of a serving dish and the potatoes on the other side. Put the blanched vegetables in the centre of the dish.

Add the lemon juice to the peanut sauce and pour it over the vegetables. Garnish with the chopped peanuts and fried onion.

This is a really refreshing salad with a bit of a kick in the tail. It can be served on its own or with fishcakes or rissoles.

A lovely crunchy salad with a spicy dressing, this would be good in winter – and it's good for you!

Thai Salad

Vegetable Salad

½ firm white cabbage, shredded

2 carrots, peeled and grated

2 spring onions, cut into very fine strips

1 fresh red chilli, deseeded and cut into very fine strips

1 tablespoon ground dried prawns (optional)

For the dressing

1 tablespoon fish sauce

2 teaspoons sugar

2 garlic cloves, peeled and crushed

2 tablespoons lime juice

freshly ground black pepper

Serves 4–6

Mix all the salad ingredients together in a large bowl.

Mix all the dressing ingredients together thoroughly in a bowl.

Pour the dressing onto the salad, toss together and serve.

½ firm white cabbage, finely shredded

5 carrots, peeled and grated

3 red onions, peeled and thinly sliced

100 g/3½ oz runner beans, thinly sliced

salt

a handful of crushed, unsalted peanuts, to garnish

For the dressing

2 small fresh red chillies, finely chopped

2.5 cm/1 inch piece of fresh ginger, peeled and finely chopped

3 garlic cloves, peeled and finely chopped

125 ml/4 fl oz groundnut oil

40 ml/1½ fl oz white wine vinegar

1 teaspoon curry powder

1 teaspoon mustard seeds, crushed

½ teaspoon turmeric powder

Mix together all the vegetables in a large bowl.

Mix together all the ingredients for the dressing and toss the vegetables in the dressing.

Season with salt, sprinkle on the peanuts and serve.

Serves 4–6

This is a summery salad dressed with Asian flavours of sesame, coriander, lime and ginger.

Not one for the faint-hearted among you. This is full of flavour, with lots of chilli.

Spicy Salad

Floyd's Salad

1 crisp lettuce, chopped

½ cucumber, peeled, deseeded and chopped into cubes

1 red onion, peeled and finely sliced

1 red pepper, deseeded and chopped into 1 cm/½ inch chunks

1 green pepper, deseeded and chopped into 1 cm/½ inch chunks

5 tomatoes, skinned, deseeded and chopped

For the dressing

4 fresh green chillies, finely chopped

1 tablespoon sesame oil

½ teaspoon coriander powder

½ teaspoon chilli powder

½ teaspoon ground ginger

juice of ½ lime

salt and freshly ground black pepper

Mix together the lettuce, cucumber, onion, peppers and tomatoes in a large bowl and season with salt.

In a small bowl, mix together all the dressing ingredients and season with salt and pepper.

Pour the dressing over the salad and toss well to coat.

Serves 4–6

3 red onions, peeled and very finely sliced

1 large fresh green chilli, deseeded and very finely sliced into strips

1 large fresh red chilli, deseeded and very finely sliced into strips

2.5 cm/1 inch piece of fresh ginger, peeled and very finely sliced into strips

1 large bunch of flat-leafed parsley, stalks removed

1 large bunch of coriander leaves, stalks removed

walnut oil

Put all the ingredients except the walnut oil in a bowl and mix. Sprinkle over the walnut oil, mix well and serve as an accompaniment.

Serves 4–6

Rice, Breads and Chutneys

This makes a change from plain rice as an accompaniment. It is a bit more substantial.

Dill is a very aromatic herb that accompanies fish dishes so well, so this rice dish is wonderful with fish or seafood kebabs.

Savoury Lentils and Rice

175 g/6 oz green lentils

350 g/12 oz long-grain rice, washed under cold running water until the water runs clear

100 g/3½ oz ghee or clarified butter

1 onion, peeled and finely chopped

2 garlic cloves, peeled and finely chopped

8 cloves

4 cardamom pods, crushed

1 cinnamon stick

1½ teaspoons turmeric powder

salt and freshly ground black pepper

Serves 8–10

Put the lentils and rice into a large bowl and soak in cold water for 2 hours.

Heat the ghee or clarified butter in a frying pan and gently fry the onion and garlic until they are soft.

Add the spices and seasonings and stir-fry for 3–4 minutes.

Drain the rice and lentils and add to the onion, garlic and spices in the pan, stirring well to make sure all the grains are coated in the mixture.

Add 900 ml/1½ pints of boiling water, bring to the boil, cover and simmer for 20–30 minutes until the grains are tender.

Remove the lid and leave on the heat, stirring constantly, until all the liquid has been absorbed. Serve immediately.

Rice with Dill

200 g/7 oz long-grain rice, washed under cold running water until the water runs clear

vegetable oil, for frying

2 green cardamom pods, crushed

1 fresh green chilli, very finely chopped

a good handful of fresh dill, finely chopped

salt

Serves 4–6

Heat a little vegetable oil in a pan, add the cardamom pods and chilli and stir-fry for about 1 minute.

Add the dill and salt to taste and sauté for 1 minute.

Add 400 ml/14 fl oz of water and bring to the boil, then add the rice and cook until all the liquid has been absorbed and the rice is tender.

Serve with your favourite fish dish.

Rice is all too often served plain, accompanying another dish;
however, it absorbs other flavours so well. This dish would stand
proudly on its own, with the addition of cashew nuts giving it texture.

Spicy Lemon Rice

300 g/11 oz long-grain rice, washed under cold running water until the water runs clear

ghee or clarified butter

vegetable oil, for frying

1 teaspoon black mustard seeds

10 fresh curry leaves

1 fresh green chilli, finely chopped

4 dried red chillies, crushed

2.5 cm/1 inch piece of fresh ginger, peeled and grated

a handful of unsalted cashew nuts

½ teaspoon turmeric powder

juice of 2 lemons

a good handful of fresh coriander leaves, chopped, to garnish

Serves 6

Boil the rice in a very large pan with plenty of salted water until tender, then drain well. Preheat the oven to 150°C/300°F/mark 2.

Drop a dollop of ghee or clarified butter into the rice and stir well. Transfer the rice to an ovenproof dish, cover with foil and keep warm in the oven.

Heat some vegetable oil in a pan, add the mustard seeds and stir them around until they crackle. Add the curry leaves, fresh and dried chillies, the ginger and cashew nuts and stir-fry for about 30 seconds.

Stir in the turmeric powder, lemon juice and a dash of water to moisten and cook for 3 minutes or so until you have a yellow gravy. Stir this into the rice until all the ingredients are combined and garnish with the chopped coriander.

An aromatic rice that goes particularly well with lamb dishes.

Spicy and slightly caramelised, this rice dish is a great accompaniment to most meat dishes.

Saffron Rice with Cumin

300 g/11 oz long-grain rice, washed under cold running water until the water runs clear

2 teaspoons cumin seeds

a pinch of saffron strands

salt

Serves 4–6

Toast the cumin seeds in a dry frying pan for a few seconds until they release their aroma.

Boil the rice with the saffron in plenty of salted water.

When the rice is cooked, drain and stir in the toasted cumin seeds.

Browned Rice

550 g/1¼ lb basmati rice, soaked for 15 minutes

vegetable oil, for frying

2 onions, peeled and finely sliced

1 cinnamon stick

1 bay leaf

5 cloves

1 teaspoon freshly grated nutmeg

2 teaspoons sugar

salt

Serves 8–10

Wash the soaked rice under lots of cold running water until the water runs clear and drain.

Heat a little vegetable oil in a pan and fry the onions until they are well browned.

Add the cinnamon, bay leaf, cloves and nutmeg and sauté for 5 minutes.

Add the sugar and allow to caramelize, but do not let it burn.

Add the rice and sauté for a couple of minutes, then season to taste and add plenty of boiling water. Cover the pan and cook for 9–10 minutes over a medium heat until the rice is tender and the water has been absorbed.

This is quite a hot rice dish, and the coconut adds a great texture to the finished item. Coconut rice is good with grilled fish or meat.

This is not the fried rice we know and love from the local restaurant. The flavours really come through!

Coconut Rice

250 g/9 oz basmati rice, soaked for 15 minutes

150 g/5 oz grated fresh coconut (if using dried, see page 85)

vegetable oil, for frying

1 teaspoon mustard seeds

5 dried red chillies, crushed

3 fresh green chillies, deseeded and finely chopped

2 garlic cloves, peeled and finely chopped

4 cardamom pods, crushed

2.5 cm/1 inch piece of fresh ginger, peeled and grated

1 teaspoon turmeric powder

10 fresh curry leaves

ghee or clarified butter

salt

a good handful of chopped fresh coriander leaves, to garnish

Wash the soaked rice under lots of cold running water until the water runs clear and drain.

Boil the rice in plenty of salted water for about 7 minutes, drain and place in a dish to dry out.

Toast the coconut in a dry frying pan until golden brown.

Heat some vegetable oil in a pan, add the mustard seeds and stir-fry for about 30 seconds, then add the dried and fresh chillies, the garlic, cardamom pods and ginger and stir-fry for another 30 seconds.

Add the turmeric and curry leaves and stir-fry for 30 seconds, then add the coconut and rice and stir-fry for 2 minutes.

Remove from the heat and cover for 1 hour to let the flavours infuse, then stir in the ghee or clarified butter.

Reheat either in the oven or on the stove, stirring occasionally, and garnish with the chopped coriander.

Serves 4–6

Fried Rice

175 g/6 oz basmati rice, washed under cold running water until the water runs clear and soaked for 30 minutes

vegetable oil, for frying

2 small red onions, peeled and finely chopped

8 cloves

4 cardamom pods, crushed

1 teaspoon cumin seeds

1 teaspoon coriander seeds

1 cinnamon stick

1 bay leaf

salt

Drain the rice and reserve the soaking water. Put both to one side.

Heat some vegetable oil in a frying pan and stir-fry the onions until they are just soft, then add all the remaining ingredients and continue sautéeing to release the flavour of the spices.

Add the rice to the pan and stir-fry for about 2 minutes until the rice is well coated with the flavourings.

Tip in enough of the soaking water to cover the rice and simmer for about 12 minutes until the water is absorbed and the rice is cooked.

Serves 3–4

This recipe is very simple, if a little time-consuming, but worth it for that authentic Indian taste.

Simple Naan Bread

350 g/12 oz strong plain white flour

1 teaspoon salt

1 teaspoon fast-acting dried yeast

1 teaspoon honey

25 g/1 oz butter, melted

Sift the flour and salt into a large bowl and sprinkle in the yeast. Make a well in the centre and add 175 ml/6 fl oz of warm water, the honey and butter and mix together well.

Knead until you have a silky dough, then cover and leave in a warm place for 1 hour until the dough has doubled in size.

Knead again to knock out the air and shape as required – either several small breads or one big one. Cover and set aside to rise for 15 minutes. Preheat the oven to 230°C/450°F/mark 8 and put a baking sheet in to heat up.

Put the risen dough on the hot baking sheet and bake for 10 or so minutes until golden brown.

In India bread is a very popular accompaniment to curry. It is used for scooping up the lovely sauces and chutneys. Flavoured with spinach, this bread makes a colourful and simple snack.

This flat bread is served all the time in India, for breakfast, lunch and dinner and for snacks throughout the day.

Spinach Bread

1 teaspoon cumin seeds

60 g/2½ oz cooked spinach with all the liquid squeezed out

250 g/9 oz wholewheat flour

salt

ghee or clarified butter, to serve

Toast the cumin seeds in a dry frying pan for a few seconds, then grind them lightly with the back of a spoon to break them up.

Mix together the cumin, spinach, flour and salt to taste and add water a little at a time to make a dough. Divide the dough into 6 separate balls and roll each flat with a rolling pin into a disc.

Toast the discs on each side in a dry frying pan until they are browned. Paint each with a little ghee or clarified butter and serve.

Roti

110 g/4 oz wholemeal flour

1 teaspoon ghee or vegetable oil

Mix the flour with 75 ml/2½ fl oz of warm water.

Add the ghee or vegetable oil and knead thoroughly for at least 7 minutes until the texture is smooth and soft. Cover and leave for 1 hour.

Shape the dough and cook in a hot dry frying pan for about 2 minutes on each side, until lightly browned.

Chutneys and salsas are so easy to make and add so much to a dish. Most chutneys will keep comfortably in the fridge for at least a week, salsas probably just for a couple of days.

Fresh Mango Chutney

2 slightly underipe mangoes, peeled and thinly sliced

a handful of chopped cashew nuts

1 fresh red chilli, finely chopped

a handful of raisins

a handful of chopped fresh mint leaves

½ teaspoon cumin powder

½ teaspoon coriander powder

1 teaspoon soft brown sugar

½ teaspoon turmeric powder

Put the mango slices into a bowl, add the rest of the ingredients and stir gently until they are thoroughly mixed. Chill in the fridge for at least 2 hours.

Serve with naan bread, poppadoms or your favourite curry.

Sweet Mango Chutney

2 large unripe mangoes, peeled and cut into small cubes

500 g/1 lb 2 oz pure cane sugar

1 tablespoon chilli powder

½ tablespoon fennel seeds

1 teaspoon fenugreek seeds

1 tablespoon white wine vinegar

a good pinch of salt

1 teaspoon small black mustard seeds

oil, for preserving

Preheat the oven to 180°C/350°F/ mark 4. Mix together all the ingredients except the mustard seeds and oil.

Put the mixture in a tight-lidded jar and cook in a bain-marie in the oven for about 1 hour until the ingredients have softened (you could also do this on top of the stove).

When the jar has cooled down, sprinkle the mustard seeds on top and cover the chutney with oil.

Seal and refrigerate for 2–3 weeks before using.

Cucumber Chutney

1 cucumber, peeled, deseeded and cut into batons

50 ml/2 fl oz white wine vinegar

2.5 cm/1 inch piece of fresh ginger, peeled and very finely diced

5 small fresh green chillies, very finely chopped

salt

Put the vinegar, salt and a dash of water into a pan and bring to the boil. While still boiling, add the ginger and cucumber and cook for a couple of minutes until the cucumber is just softening.

Bring off the heat, pop into a clean jar or bowl and stir in the green chillies. Refrigerate overnight before using.

Sweet and Sour Chutney

6 tablespoons grated fresh coconut (if using dried, see page 85)

a large bunch of coriander leaves

2.5 cm/1 inch piece of fresh ginger, peeled and finely chopped

6 fresh green chillies

4 garlic cloves, peeled

1 teaspoon coriander seeds

a dash of white wine vinegar

sugar

salt

Place all the ingredients except the sugar and salt into a food processor and whiz to a smooth paste. Add sugar and salt to taste.

Beetroot Raita

6 cooked baby beetroots (not in vinegar), peeled

300 ml/½ pint tub of natural yoghurt

1 teaspoon sugar

a handful of finely chopped chives, plus extra to garnish

a pinch of cayenne pepper

salt

Cut the beetroot into thin slices and arrange in a serving dish.

Mix together the yoghurt, sugar, chives, cayenne pepper and salt and chill in the fridge for 30 minutes.

Pour the yoghurt mixture over the beetroot slices and garnish with more chopped chives.

Coriander and Mint Chutney

a large handful of fresh coriander leaves

a large handful of fresh mint leaves

2 apples, peeled, cored and cut into cubes

Whiz all the ingredients together in a food processor until you have a wonderfully aromatic paste.

Spicy Lime Pickle

10–12 limes, cut into wedges

3 teaspoons fenugreek seeds

3 teaspoons mustard seeds

5 teaspoons chilli powder

1 fresh green chilli, finely chopped

3 teaspoons turmeric powder

250–270 ml/ 8½–9 fl oz vegetable oil

salt

Put the lime wedges into a bowl, sprinkle with salt and leave for 10–15 minutes.

Roast the fenugreek and mustard seeds in a dry frying pan for a minute or so to release their aromas, then grind to a powder in a pestle and mortar.

Add the chilli powder, fresh chilli and turmeric powder and mix well, then sprinkle this mixture over the limes and stir all the ingredients together.

Add the vegetable oil, cover the bowl with a dry cloth and leave in a warm place for about a week. Then put the pickle into jars and store in the fridge for about 2 weeks before using.

Coconut Chutney

225 g/8 oz grated fresh coconut (or, if you are using dried coconut, soak it for 1 hour in a little coconut milk)

4 tablespoons white lentils, rinsed and drained

6 fresh green chillies

2 fresh red chillies

2.5 cm/1 inch piece of fresh ginger, peeled

1 teaspoon black mustard seeds

a little coconut milk

10–12 fresh curry leaves

Gently roast the white lentils in a dry frying pan, being careful not to burn them.

Put the lentils with all the other ingredients except the curry leaves into a food processor and blend thoroughly, softening with enough coconut milk to make a paste.

Tip into a bowl and mix in the curry leaves. Refrigerate until needed.

Tomato Chutney

400 g/14 oz cherry tomatoes, cut into quarters

4–6 spring onions, chopped

1 fresh green chilli, finely chopped

a handful of fresh coriander leaves, chopped

a dash of lemon juice

a pinch of cayenne pepper

salt

Mix the tomatoes with the spring onions, chilli, coriander leaves and salt to taste.

Stir gently together, then add a squeeze of lemon juice and the cayenne pepper. Mix once more, cover and place in the fridge for at least 1 hour before using.

Raita

chopped mint

diced tomato

diced cucumber

chopped fresh chillies

chopped spring onions

natural yoghurt

Mix any or all of the ingredients with enough natural yoghurt to make a dropping consistency.

Spicy Hot Cucumber, Tomato and Chilli Relish

12.5 cm/5 inch chunk of cucumber, peeled, deseeded and finely chopped

2 large tomatoes, skinned, deseeded and finely chopped

2 fresh green chillies, finely chopped

1 red onion, peeled and finely chopped

½ teaspoon chilli powder

a handful of fresh coriander leaves, finely chopped

juice of 2 or 3 limes

salt

Mix all the ingredients together in a large bowl and place in the fridge for about 30 minutes. Use on the same day.

Sweet Chilli Sauce

10 fresh green chillies, deseeded and chopped

4 garlic cloves, peeled

1 tablespoon fish sauce

juice of 2 limes

2 shallots, peeled

1 tablespoon runny honey

Briefly whiz all the ingredients in a food processor – not too finely, so that you can still make out the ingredients. Spoon into a bowl and serve.

Index